UNRAVELING
REVELATION

UNRAVELING
REVELATION

STEPPING INTO 7 ROOMS OF INSIGHT

MARILYN HICKEY

WHITAKER
HOUSE

UNRAVELING REVELATION:
Stepping into Seven Rooms of Insight
(Previously published as *The New Millennium and End Time Propecy* and *The Book of Revelation*.)

Marilyn Hickey Ministries
P.O. Box 6598
Englewood, CO 80155-6598
www.marilynandsarah.org

ISBN: 978-1-62911-956-4
eBook ISBN: 978-1-62911-957-1
Printed in the United States of America
© 1987, 1989, 1999, 2012, 2018 by Marilyn Hickey Ministries

Whitaker House
1030 Hunt Valley Circle
New Kensington, PA 15068
www.whitakerhouse.com

1 2 3 4 5 6 7 8 9 10 11 ⨄ 25 24 23 22 21 20 19 18

Write the things which you have seen, and the things which are,
and the things which shall be hereafter.
—Jesus

Revelation 1:19

CONTENTS

INTRODUCTION

The book of Revelation is a closed book to most Christians, but God wants it to be *revealed* to us.

An angel told John (the human author of Revelation):

The apostle John wrote Revelation while banished on the Isle of Patmos. John calls himself the *servant* of Jesus Christ. An angel told John,

> *Seal not the sayings of the prophecy of this book: for the time is at hand.* (Revelation 22:10)

The Bible, in fact, promises us a blessing if we read this book:

> *Blessed is he that reads, and they that hear the words of this prophecy, and keep those things which are written therein: for the time is at hand.* (Revelation 1:3)

We are going to study the book of Revelation together, and we are going to do what was prophesied to Daniel:

> *But you, O Daniel, shut up the words, and seal the book, even to the time of the end: many*

shall run to and fro, and knowledge shall be increased.   (Daniel 12:4)

The portion of this Hebrew Scripture that says, *"many shall run to and fro"* basically means "to walk through the pages with your fingers."

Some of you will remember the advertising slogan for the Yellow Pages found in phone books: "Let your fingers do the walking." I used to chuckle when I thought of how God had a jump on Madison Avenue. I want you, with your own fingers, to walk through the pages of the book of Revelation with me. And as we walk through the pages of this book, *"knowledge shall be increased,"* just as was promised to Daniel.

I want you to do some comparing of the New and Old Testament Scriptures as we go through our study. I believe that, as we compare Scripture with Scripture, as the Holy Spirit tells us to do in 1 Corinthians 2:13, this book will open up to us. We will open up to God's Word, and God will do a mighty work in us and bless us for being involved in this wonderful study.

The book of Revelation is deeply rooted in the Old Testament; there is little in it that is "new." We are shown the Lord's grand plan to take over the kingdoms of this world and make them the kingdom of God.

John was *"in the Spirit"* (Revelation 1:10) when he received this revelation. My prayer is that the Holy Spirit will lead us to truth as we study together, and that we will also be "in the Spirit."

In this study, we will follow the outline that was given to John:

Write the things which you have seen, and the things which are, and the things which shall be hereafter.   (Revelation 1:19)

We will behold *"the thing which you have seen,"* as found in chapter 1. We will behold Jesus. In the past, we have seen Him as a man of sorrow and acquainted with grief, but now we will see the risen and glorified Christ, who is Lord of Lords and King of Kings, and our own personal Savior.

Then we will also look at *"the things which are,"* found in chapters 2 and 3. We will study the letters to the seven churches in Asia and discover how they basically depict conditions in the seven church ages.

Finally, we will look at *"the things which shall be hereafter."* We will look into the future. Revelation reveals that the ultimate winners are the Christians.

Here are some points to keep in mind that will help us on our walk through Revelation:

1. Remember that this book is a prophetic book. It concerns some things that are past and some that were present at the time of writing, but it mostly deals with things that will shortly come to pass.

2. I believe Revelation is a book that has a divine order, and we are going to discover that orderly sequence. Otherwise, we will remain hopelessly confused.

3. There are three major books about prophecy:

   a. Daniel

   b. Ezekiel

   c. Revelation

As a continuation of the book of Acts, the book of Revelation admonishes us again and again to hear what the Spirit is saying to the churches:

He that has an ear, let him hear what the Spirit says to the churches; to him that overcomes will I

_____

_____

_____

_____

_____

_____

_____

_____

_____

_____

_____

_____

_____

_____

_____

_____

_____

_____

_____

_____

_____

_____

_____

_____

give to eat of the tree of life, which is in the midst of the paradise of God. (Revelation 2:7)

He that has an ear, let him hear what the Spirit says to the churches; He that overcomes shall not be hurt of the second death. (Revelation 2:11)

He that has an ear, let him hear what the Spirit says to the churches; to him that overcomes will I give to eat of the hidden manna, and will give him a white stone, and in the stone a new name written, which no man knows saving he that receives it. (Revelation 2:17)

He that has an ear, let him hear what the Spirit says to the churches. (Revelation 2:29)

He that has an ear, let him hear what the Spirit says to the churches. (Revelation 3:6)

He that has an ear, let him hear what the Spirit says to the churches. (Revelation 13)

He that has an ear, let him hear what the Spirit says to the churches. (Revelation 22)

4. The Greek word *apokalupsis* is sometimes translated as *revelation*. It means "the removing of the veil, unveiling, disclosure, appearing, coming, manifestation."

5. The basic themes of Revelation are *redemption* and *regeneration*. The concept of *redemption* is to restore something to its original owner; whereas *regeneration*, the second theme of Revelation, is to restore something to its original state. *Redemption* refers to man's soul, man's body, the human race, and the

earth. Jesus, the Lamb of God, became the Redeemer through His suffering and death.

We are in the day of redemption of the soul; the redemption of the *earth* and the *body* are yet to come in the future:

And when these things begin to come to pass, then look up, and lift up your heads; for your redemption draws near. (Luke 21:28)
[This is redemption of the body.]

And not only they, but ourselves also, which have the first-fruits of the Spirit, even we ourselves groan inside ourselves, waiting for the adoption, that is, the redemption of our body.
(Romans 8:23)

And grieve not the Holy Spirit of God, whereby you are sealed to the day of redemption.
(Ephesians 4:30)

Notice that when Jesus spoke of the catching away (the rapture), He called it, *"your redemption."*

The story of man is summed up in three words beginning with *generation* as seen in Genesis chapters one and two. Beginning in Genesis chapter three, we would have to use the word *degeneration*. Finally, in the New Testament, because of the new birth, we can say *regeneration*. Remember, anything that is *regenerated* has first been through the process of *degeneration*.

Regeneration appears twice in our Bibles. *Once* it has to do with the soul:

Not by works of righteousness which we have done, but according to His mercy He saved us, by the washing of regeneration, and renewing of the Holy Ghost. (Titus 3:5)

Once it has to do with the earth:

Verily I say to you, That you which have followed Me, in the regeneration when the Son of Man shall sit in the throne of His glory, you also shall sit upon twelve thrones, judging the twelve tribes of Israel. (Matthew 19:28)

It is easy to see that regeneration would not apply to our bodies because that would mean going back to our original state and being subject to death again. Instead, we get a "glorified" body:

And if children, then heirs; heirs of God, and joint-heirs with Christ; if so be that we suffer with Him, that we may be also glorified together. For I reckon that the sufferings of this present time are not worthy to be compared with the glory which shall be revealed in us.

(Romans 8:17–18)

It is sown a natural body; it is raised a spiritual body. There is a natural body, and there is a spiritual body. (1 Corinthians 15:44)

6. There are two purifying agents that God uses in redemption because redemption has to do with cleansing: one is blood and the other is fire. We are redeemed by the blood of Christ. The earth will be redeemed by fire. Some things cannot be redeemed by blood or fire: Satan's church, Satan's man (the Antichrist), Satan's kingdom, and, of course, Satan himself.

7. One of the purposes of going through this book is to alert God's people to the time we are living in, and to help them understand what Jesus is saying to the church today. We

will see this especially in chapters two and three.

8. There are many *symbols* in this book. Throughout the Bible, we see symbols: for example, leaven was used as a symbol of evil in the Old Testament (see Exodus 12:15) and used as a symbol of resurrection in the New Testament (see Luke 24:34–35). Jesus taught in parables and used many symbols in teaching about the kingdom. In Matthew chapter 13, *seeds* are a symbol of the Word of God, *fowls* are a symbol of the "wicked one," and the *ground* is symbolic of the heart of the hearer. We see also that *tares* are a symbol of godless people and *wheat* is a symbol of godly people. (See Matthew 13:38.) Of course, we all know that the *dove* is the symbol of the Holy Spirit and that the "Bread of Life" refers to Jesus.

    In Revelation, we will see candlesticks and stars representing churches and messengers. We will see a woman and a man child representing God's people. We will see Satan pictured as a dragon; we will see beasts; we will see the false church pictured as a scarlet woman. Of course, we will also see that much of the book will actually be fulfilled literally.

9. Jesus Christ appears under various names in this book. Those names are given to Him according to the work that He does in different circumstances. Sometimes He is called an Angel, sometimes a Lion, and sometimes a Lamb.

10. We will see that the saints are constantly singing redemption songs. It is amazing to see how many songs are in the book of Revelation!

11. Revelation uses numbers a great deal. Here is a quick look at their significance: *one* is the number of God (see Deuteronomy 6:4), *three* represents the Trinity, *four* has to do with the world (because of the four directions), *six* is the number of evil (it is Satan's number—see Revelation 13:18; Daniel 3:1), *seven* has to do with completeness, *ten* shows specific happenings, and *twelve* has to do primarily with those who are redeemed.

12. Revelation is the wrap-up of His-story. The book of Genesis is the seed plot of the Bible—it is a book of beginnings—and Revelation is the book of endings. In Genesis, we see four major prophecies of Jesus.

   a. We see that He is the seed of woman prophesied in Genesis chapter three:

      And I will put enmity between you and the woman, and between your seed and her seed; it shall bruise your head, and you shall bruise his heel. (Genesis 3:15)

   b. We see that He will come forth from the lineage of Shem in Genesis chapter nine. From Shem would come the Jews, who would be the bearer of the name "Messiah" to the world. It will be Shem, Noah's seed, through whom the name of all names will come. Shem even means "name":

      And he said, Blessed be the LORD God of Shem; and Canaan shall be his servant. God shall enlarge Japheth, and he shall dwell in the tents of Shem; and Canaan shall be his servant.
      (Genesis 9:26–27)

c. We see that He is the seed (singular) of Abraham:

> *And I will bless them that bless you, and curse him that curses you: and in you shall all families of the earth be blessed.* (Genesis 12:3)

> *And Abraham said, my son, God will provide Himself a lamb for a burnt offering: so they went both of them together.... And Abraham called the name of that place Jehovah-jireh: as it is said to this day, In the mount of the* LORD *it shall be seen.* (Genesis 22:8, 14)

> *Now to Abraham and his seed were the promises made. He said not, And to seeds, as of many; but as of one, And to your seed, which is Christ.* (Galatians 3:16)

d. We see that He is the seed (singular) of Abraham:

> *The scepter shall not depart from Judah, nor a lawgiver from between his feet, until Shiloh come; and to him shall the gathering of the people be.* (Genesis 49:10)

Every truth that we see in seed form in Genesis has its harvest in the book of Revelation. In Genesis, we see that man was given dominion over the earth but lost it. In Revelation, we see that man will inherit the earth.

In Genesis, God gave man the tree of life from which to eat. After the fall, man lost the right to eat from the tree of life, but the tree of life is growing again in Revelation. This time, however, it is also for the healing of the nations. There is no question that Satan appears to be victorious in the beginning of Genesis, but in Revelation, he appears and is absolutely defeated. (See chart on page 23.)

13. Revelation was written by John on the Isle of Patmos through the inspiration of the Holy Spirit. The Isle of Patmos is in the Mediterranean Sea, southwest of the city of Ephesus. Patmos is a rocky island about ten miles in length. I have visited the monastery of Saint John, which is on a hill overlooking the island. Near the citadel, there is a grotto where John is supposed to have received the vision of Revelation.

God promises a *blessing* to those who read the book of Revelation. The word *blessing* means "happy." The book of Revelation is meant to be a source of happiness!

In AD 95, during the reign of the Roman emperor Domitian, John was banished to the Isle of Patmos. Eighteen months later, under the reign of Nerva, he was released. It was during this period of imprisonment that John received the Revelation.

Many traditions have come down concerning the events in the latter days of John's life. Tertullian, a famous writer of the early fathers, declared that John was banished to Patmos after he had miraculously survived immersion in boiling oil. It is believed that John lived until AD 98.

AN OVERVIEW

Remember, God's major goal is not finished until the whole world is in its original state and back to its original Owner. Christ must reign until all enemies are put under His feet:

For He has put all things under His feet.
(1 Corinthians 15:25)

Once that is accomplished, the saints will reign with Him and will judge the inhabitants of the world:

Do you not know that the saints shall judge the world? and if the world shall be judged by you, are you unworthy to judge the smallest matters?
(1 Corinthians 6:2)

For to the angels has He not put in subjection the world to come, whereof we speak. But one in a certain place testified, saying, What is man, that You are mindful of him? or the son of man, that You visit him? You made him a little lower than the angels; You crowned him with glory and honor, and did set him over the works of Your hands: You have put all things in subjection under his feet. For in that He put all in subjection under him, He left nothing that is not put under him. But now we see not yet all things put under him. But we see Jesus, who was made a little lower than the angels for the suffering of death, crowned with glory and honor; that He by the grace of God should taste death for every man. (Hebrews 2:5–9)

In the meantime the preaching of the Word and the program of redemption is committed to the Body of Christ; we are a part of God's grand plan of redemption.

Revelation can be conceptualized as a house with seven rooms, three of which describe parallel events from different perspectives. Let's look at a quick overview of all seven rooms before starting our study in detail. (See chart on page 23.)

ROOM ONE

In the first room of Revelation (chapter one), there is a beautiful picture of Jesus Christ as Prophet, Priest, Judge, and King. He is well qualified to be our Redeemer.

ROOM TWO

The second room of Revelation (chapters two and three) refers primarily to the church and to church history. I personally believe these descriptions of the local churches picture a history of the church ages.

ROOM THREE

There is a "door" from this second room that opens into the third room, where we see the scene of what is going on in heaven immediately after the rapture. We will see events on earth, but from a *heavenly* perspective in chapters 4–11.

ROOM FOUR

Another "door" from the second room opens into the fourth room, which shows the Antichrist and those who are left behind after the rapture. This section is comprised of chapters 12–16 and parallels chapters 4–11.

ROOM FIVE

A final "door" from the second room opens downward to the fifth room. Here we see the satanic church, which has its earthly expression through a woman called Jezebel of the Thyatira church (see Revelation 2:20–24) and the harlot woman of chapter 17. Chapters 17 and 18 provide additional details to the happenings of the previous two rooms.

Notice that rooms three, four, and five are parallel. These three scenes occur simultaneously; they are related one to another, the same items appear in all three, but each has a different viewpoint: one is from heaven, one is from earth, and one is from Satan's viewpoint. Keep this fact in mind as we study Revelation, and you will avoid much confusion.

The third room (chapters 4–11) contains John's vision of God's throne, the seven-sealed book, and the seven trumpet judgments. Keep in mind that this room covers the time from the rapture until the return of Christ with the saints (us!) to destroy the wicked kings of the earth at Armageddon.

The fourth room (chapters 12–16) shows us primarily what is happening on the earth after the rapture. There is much symbolic language here. In this segment, we look down on the earth and see things happening as a result of the activities in heaven. Next we are on the earth to see the man child caught up to heaven. Then we see the persecution of the Antichrist and the conflict of the armies of the world against the Lord.

The fifth room (chapters 17 and 18) follows the activities of the false church of Satan. We see the mystery of evil and its final destruction. There is no outlet from this room—everything will be destroyed.

ROOM SIX

Room six (chapters 19 and 20) describes the kingdom age. There is a great wedding in heaven that involves the saints. They are united as the bride of Christ, and will reign with Him during the millennium and forever. At the end of this thousand-year period, Satan prepares for a final battle. Fire from heaven devours his followers, and he is cast into the lake of fire.

ROOM SEVEN

The seventh room (chapters 21 and 22) ushers us into the very presence of God, the eternal home of the saints. Eye hasn't seen, nor ear heard, nor has it entered into the heart of man, all the wonderful things that God has for us in that day. Remember, however, that the Spirit reveals them to us:

> *But as it is written, Eye has not seen, nor ear heard, neither have entered into the heart of man, the things which God has prepared for them that love Him. But God has revealed them to us by His Spirit: for the Spirit searches all things, yea, the deep things of God.*
>
> (1 Corinthians 2:9–10)

When you walk through the seven rooms, as if walking through the seven rooms of a house, you see the plan and purpose of the end times for yourself. Look up, because your redemption is drawing near! There are many things too wonderful for us to grasp. And yet, we are a picture people and can sometimes understand with our eyes what is hidden to our mind. As God pictures this house with seven rooms in your heart, remember that God loves you into eternity with an extravagant love.

Revelation completes the truths that began in Genesis:

Genesis shows man's fall from Paradise.

Revelation shows man restored to Paradise.

Genesis tells of the beginning of man's rebellion.

Revelation tells of the end of man's rebellion.

Genesis tells of the beginning of the curse.

Revelation says that there will be no more curse.

Genesis tells of the first death.

Revelation promises that there will be no more death.

Genesis tells that Satan's head will be bruised.

Revelation shows Satan bruised and judged.

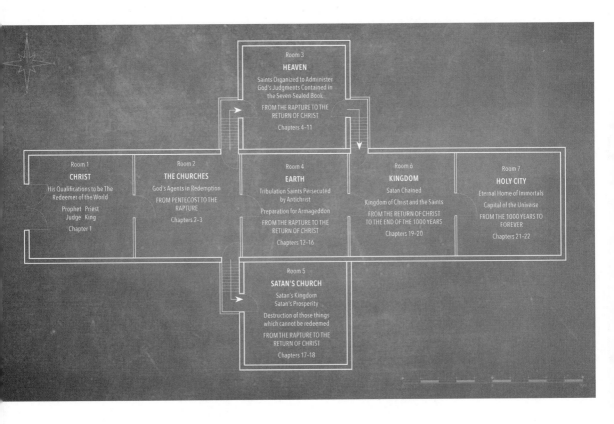

CHAPTER ONE

Let's go back to section one now and begin our detailed study of this marvelous book. John begins by giving us a highly symbolic description of Jesus as Prophet, Priest, Judge, and King.

Throughout the four Gospels, Jesus is seen as the Prophet spoken of by Moses:

> The LORD your God will raise up to you a Prophet from the midst of you, of your brethren, like to me; to Him you shall hearken.... I will raise them up a Prophet from among their brethren, like to you, and will put My words in his mouth; and he shall speak to them all that I shall command him. And it shall come to pass, that whosoever will not hearken to My words which he shall speak in My name, I will require it of him. (Deuteronomy 18:15, 18–19)

Jesus is also our Priest. He became our Savior, and so He stands among the candlesticks, clothed with His priestly robe showing His priestly and sacrificial work:

> But Christ being come a high priest of good things to come, by a greater and more perfect

REVELATION 1

[1]The Revelation of Jesus Christ, which God gave to Him, to show to His servants things which must shortly come to pass; and He sent and signified it by His angel to His servant John:

[2]who bore record of the word of God, and of the testimony of Jesus Christ, and of all things that he saw.

[3]Blessed is he that reads, and they that hear the words of this prophecy, and keep those things which are written therein: for the time is at hand.

[4]John to the seven churches which are in Asia: Grace be to you, and peace, from Him which is, and which was, and which is to come; and from the seven Spirits which are before His throne;

[5]and from Jesus Christ, who is the faithful witness, and the First Begotten of the dead, and the Prince of the kings of the earth. To Him that loved us, and washed us from our sins in His own blood,

[6]and has made us kings and priests to God and His Father; to Him be glory and dominion for ever and ever. Amen.

[7]Behold, He comes with clouds; and every eye shall see Him, and they also which pierced Him: and all kindreds of the earth shall wail because of Him. Even so, Amen.

[8]I am Alpha and Omega, the beginning and the ending, says the Lord,

which is, and which was, and which is to come, the Almighty.

⁹I John, who also am your brother, and companion in tribulation, and in the kingdom and patience of Jesus Christ, was in the isle that is called Patmos, for the word of God, and for the testimony of Jesus Christ.

¹⁰I was in the Spirit on the Lord's day, and heard behind me a great voice, as of a trumpet,

¹¹Saying, I am Alpha and Omega, the first and the last: and, What you see, write in a book, and send it to the seven churches which are in Asia; to Epheus, and to Smyrna, and to Pergamos, and to Thyatira, and to Sardis, and to Philadelphia, and to Laodicea.

¹²And I turned to see the voice that spoke with me. And being turned, I saw seven golden candlesticks;

¹³and in the midst of the seven candlesticks one like to the Son of man, clothed with a garment down to the foot, and girt about the breasts with a golden girdle.

¹⁴His head and His hairs were white like wool, as white as snow; and His eyes were as a flame of fire;

¹⁵and His feet like to fine brass, as if they burned in a furnace; and His voice as the sound of many waters.

¹⁶And He had in His right hand seven stars: and out of His mouth went a sharp two edged sword: and His countenance was as the sun shines in His strength.

tabernacle, not made with hands, that is to say, not of this building.… How much more shall the blood of Christ, who through the eternal Spirit offered Himself without spot to God, purge your conscience from dead works to serve the living God? (Hebrews 9:11, 14)

He is the Judge; He will reward His servants and punish His enemies. Tribulation will come upon the world, and He will judge the nations:

For the Father judges no man, but has committed all judgment to the Son. (John 5:22)

He is also a King—the King of Kings:

That you keep this commandment without spot, unrebukable, until the appearing of our Lord Jesus Christ: which in His times He shall show, who is the blessed and only Potentate, the King of kings, and Lord of lords.
(1 Timothy 6:14–15)

Wherever Christ is mentioned throughout the book, you will usually find some part of His description is taken from this first chapter. Remember, He is Prophet, Priest, Judge, and King.

John saw Christ "*in the midst of the seven candlesticks,*" holding seven stars in His right hand. This description reminds us of Christ's promise to the church:

For where two or three are gathered together in My name, there am I in the midst of them.
(Matthew 18:20)

We are told that the seven stars are the angels or messengers of the seven churches. The headship of the church is always with Jesus Christ.

The vital key to understanding the proper outline of this book is in verse 19:

Write the things which you have seen, and the things which are, and the things which shall be hereafter. (Revealtion 1:19)

"The things which thou host seen…" is a reference to the vision of Christ in chapter one.

"The things which are…" is in reference to the admonitions to the seven churches in the year around AD 95.

"The things which shall be hereafter" refers, of course, to future events.

[17]And when I saw Him, I fell at His feet as dead. And He laid His right hand upon me, saying to me, Fear not; I am the First and the Last:

[18]I am He that lives, and was dead; and, behold, I am alive for evermore, Amen; and have the keys of hell and of death.

[19]Write the things which you have seen, and the things which are, and the things which shall be hereafter;

[20]the mystery of the seven stars which you saw in My right hand, and the seven golden candlesticks. The seven stars are the angels of the seven churches: and the seven candlesticks which you saw are the seven churches.

NOTES

_____
_____
_____
_____
_____
_____
_____
_____
_____
_____
_____
_____
_____
_____

CHAPTER TWO

Christ's letters to the seven churches in Asia were addressed to churches that actually existed at that time. They are also, however, a picture of conditions within the church down through the whole church dispensation. We call this a double fulfillment of Scripture, and here are the church ages which the seven churches represent. (See chart on page 55.)

1. Ephesus—church of the apostolic age—AD 96.

2. Smyrna—chruch of the persecution beginning around the second century—AD 97.

3. Pergamos—church of imperial favor—beginning around AD 312.

4. Thyatira—church of the Papacy—beginning around AD 450.

5. Sardis—church of the Reformation—beginning around AD 1517.

6. Philadelphia—church of the latter-day outpouring—present day through the end of the age.

7. Laodicea—lukewarm church—present day through the end of the age.

REVELATION 2

¹To the angel of the church of Ephesus write; These things says He that holds the seven stars in His right hand, who walks in the midst of the seven golden candlesticks;

²I know your works, and your labor, and your patience, and how you can not bear them which are evil: and you have tried them which say they are apostles, and are not, and have found them liars:

³and have borne, and have patience, and for My name's sake have labored, and have not fainted.

⁴Nevertheless I have something against you, because you have left your first love.

⁵Remember therefore from where you are fallen, and repent, and do the first works; or else I will come to you quickly, and will remove your candlestick out of its place, except you repent.

⁶But this you have, that you hate the deeds of the Nicolaitans, which I also hate.

⁷He that has an ear, let him hear what the Spirit says to the churches; To him that overcomes will I give to eat of the tree of life, which is in the midst of the paradise of God.

———————————————

———————————————

———————————————

———————————————

In every church, Jesus *commended* them, *condemned* them, *counseled* them, and *challenged* them.

The church is to be a light to the world and is founded on the acknowledgment of Jesus as Christ, the Son of God.

> *And Simon Peter answered and said, You are the Christ, the Son of the living God. And Jesus answered and said to him,… Upon this rock I will build My church; and the gates of hell shall not prevail against it.* (Matthew 16:16–18)

THE SEVEN CHURCHES OF REVELATION

(refer to map on page 31)

EPHESUS
REVELATION 2:1-7 MISSIONARY

Let's look in more detail at the church of Ephesus. The term *apostles* in Revelation 2:2 indicates that this represents the apostolic age. This was an age with Holy Ghost ministry and the manifestation of the gifts of the Spirit. The church of Ephesus is the only church of the seven which we know for sure was founded by an apostle. (See Acts 19:1, 8.) Paul resided there for three years and founded the strong mother-church of Asia Minor. *Ephesus* means "the desired one." Fervent evangelism went on during this age.

Jesus *commended* this church:

> *I know your works, and your labor, and your patience, and how you can not bear them which are evil: and you have tried them which say they are apostles, and are not, and have found them liars: and have borne, and have patience, and for My name's sake have labored, and have not fainted.* (Revelation 2–3)

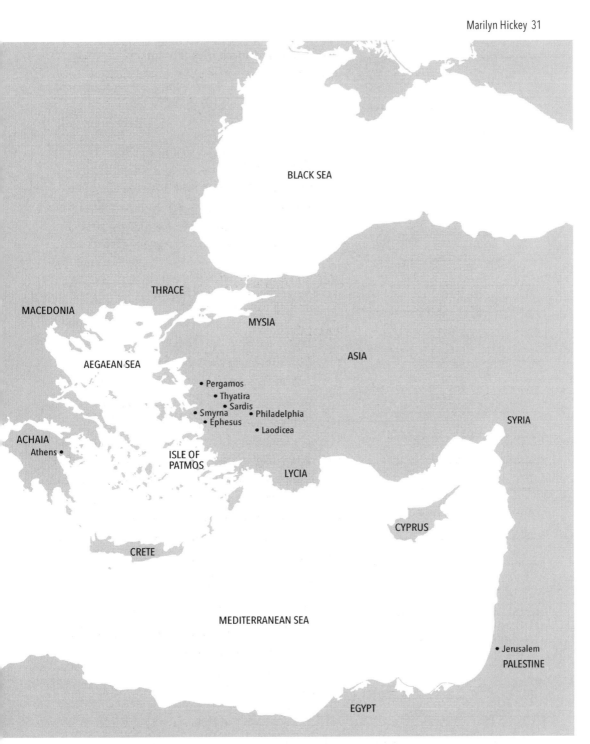

THE SEVEN CHURCHES OF THE BOOK OF REVELATION

———————————

———————————

———————————

———————————

———————————

———————————

———————————

———————————

———————————

———————————

———————————

———————————

———————————

———————————

———————————

———————————

———————————

———————————

———————————

———————————

———————————

———————————

———————————

Jesus *condemned* this church:

Nevertheless I have something against you, because you have left your first love.

(Revelation 2:4)

Jesus *counseled* this church:

Remember therefore from where you are fallen, and repent, and do the first works; or else I will come to you quickly, and will remove your candlestick out of its place, except you repent.

(Revelation 2:5)

Jesus *challenged* this church:

He that has an ear, let him hear what the Spirit says to the churches; To him that overcomes will I give to eat of the tree of life, which is in the midst of the paradise of God. (Revelation 2:7)

John tells us *how* we're to overcome:

For whatsoever is born of God overcomes the world: and this is the victory that overcomes the world, even our faith. Who is he that overcomes the world, but he that believes that Jesus is the Son of God? (1 John 5:4–5)

Historically, Ephesus was of outstanding political importance. It was known as a free city—it governed itself, independent of outside influence. It was the site of the temple of Diana of the Ephesians. This was a pretentious structure, and it was their great pride. The temple was probably 425 feet long, 220 feet wide, and 60 feet high. There were 127 pillars, each a gift of the king, all of them made of beautiful Parian marble. The inner shrine was the great altar bearing the image of Diana, which the Ephesians said fell from heaven. Their worship was hysterical and weird. Ephesus had become a haven for every kind of criminal and fugitive.

Today, Ephesus is in utter ruin. The temple of Diana, which was once one of the seven wonders of the ancient world, can hardly be identified in the desolation. It was destroyed in AD 401. The desolation is complete. Ephesus is certainly a picture of what happens to those who leave their first love.

In Paul's day, however, the church was a tremendous testimony for Jesus Christ. After certain disciples were water baptized there in the name of the Lord Jesus, they received the baptism of the Holy Spirit with speaking in other tongues. (See Acts 19:5–6.) Ephesus was a church with outstanding miracles. (See Acts 19:11–12.) It was also a church persecuted for its single-minded devotion to Christ. Ephesus was also a church where the *full* gospel was preached: Paul said he kept nothing back that was profitable unto them. (See Acts 20:20.) Ephesus was warned of apostasy and the day when grievous wolves would enter. (See Acts 20:29.) And Ephesus was the church to whom Paul wrote his most profound epistle, the letter to the Ephesians.

Before it lost its first love, Ephesus was the kind of church that we need to be in our day. They labored patiently; they did not tolerate evil in the church, and worldly men were not allowed to hold office in the assembly. Those who sought to exalt themselves were judged and exposed. The Christians had been faithful to the cause and had not grown weary in well-doing. But they became spiritually cold. We can see that Paul must have sensed this due to his warning:

For I know this, that after my departing shall grievous wolves enter in among you, not sparing the flock. Also of your own selves shall men arise, speaking perverse things, to draw away disciples after them. Therefore watch, and remember, that by the space of three years I ceased not to warn

REVELATION 2

[8]And to the angel of the church in Smyrna write; These things says the First and the Last, which was dead, and is alive;

[9]I know your works, and tribulation, and poverty, (but you are rich) and I know the blasphemy of them which say they are Jews, and are not, but are the synagogue of Satan.

[10]Fear none of those things which you shall suffer: behold, the devil shall cast some of you into prison, that you may be tried; and you shall have tribulation ten days: be you faithful to death, and I will give you a crown of life.

[11]He that has an ear, let him hear what the Spirit says to the churches; He that overcomes shall not be hurt of the second death.

NOTES

—————————————

—————————————

—————————————

—————————————

—————————————

—————————————

—————————————

—————————————

every one night and day with tears.

(Acts 20:29–31)

SMYRNA

REVELATION 2:8-11 PERSECUTION

Next is the church of Smyrna, the church of persecution, which escalated during the second century. Smyrna was a noted city located 35 miles north of Ephesus. It was very beautiful, well planned, and had a great deal of pagan temples. Politically, it was pro-Roman, and the emperors didn't forget it. It was one of the great centers of emperor worship.

At the time that John was on Patmos, during the reign of Domitian, Caesar worship, or emperor worship, was compulsory. Once a year, each Roman citizen had to burn incense on the altar to Caesar, for which he was given a commendation. Christians who refused to do this were imprisoned. Thus, the persecution began, resulting in many martyrs. Polycarp—noted Christian father and bishop of Smyrna—confessed freely that he was a Christian and was given his choice to sacrifice to Caesar or be burned. His immortal reply was, "Eighty and six years have I served Christ, and He has never done me wrong. How can I blaspheme my King who saved me?"

In AD 168, wood was gathered, and as the flames licked his body, he prayed this prayer: "I thank Thee that Thou has graciously thought me worthy of this day and this hour that I may receive a portion in the number of the martyrs in the cup of Thy Christ."

Jesus *commended* this church:

I know your works, and tribulation, and poverty, (but you are rich) and I know the blasphemy of them which say they are Jews, and are not, but are the synagogue of Satan. (Revelation 2:9)

Those who were of the *"synagogue of Satan"* were involved in two basic heresies: (1) not understanding the deity of Christ, and (2) mixing law and grace.

No word of *condemnation* was given to Smyrna.

Jesus *counseled* this church:

Fear none of those things which you shall suffer: behold, the devil shall cast some of you into prison, that you may be tried; and you shall have tribulation ten days: be you faithful to death, and I will give you a crown of life. (Revelation 2:10)

Jesus *challenged* this church:

He that has an ear, let him hear what the Spirit says to the churches; He that overcomes shall not be hurt of the second death. (Revelation 2:11)

Smyrna, modern day Izmir, is a city of about 3.03 million inhabitants and is the seaport capital of a Turkish province—a commercial center of some importance.

Once again, Jesus had said to them:

Fear none of those things which you shall suffer: behold, the devil shall cast some of you into prison, that you may be tried; and you shall have tribulation ten days: be you faithful to death, and I will give you a crown of life. (Revelation 2: 10)

The church of Smyrna represents a period of great persecution from the year AD 97 to AD 312. At John's death (AD 98), a severe persecution began, which was to continue for two centuries. It began with Domitian and was carried on by successive rulers. Caesar worship was found to be a means of unifying the empire and was required by law. The Christians were severely persecuted because they did not comply.

To the martyrs of Smyrna, Christ gave encouragement by speaking of Himself as *"the First and the Last, which was dead, and is alive"* (Revelation 2:8). Such a salutation was very appropriate to those who were experiencing martyrdom.

The name *Smyrna* means "myrrh." Myrrh was used in the burial of Christ. It is a fragrant spice which is beaten into fine pieces so it can give off its fragrance. It is a clear picture of the Christians of that day.

The *"tribulation ten days"* (Revelation 2:10) promised to this church probably referred to the ten major persecutions under the following emperors:

1. Nero: AD 54–68—Paul beheaded and Peter crucified

2. Domitian: AD 81–96—John exiled to Patmos

3. Trajan: AD 98–117—Ignatius burned at the stake

4. Marcus Aurelius: AD 161–180—Justin Martyr killed

5. Severus: AD 193–211

6. Maximinus: AD 235–238

7. Decius: AD 249–251

8. Valerian: AD 253–260

9. Aurelian: AD 270–275

10. Diocletian: AD 284–300

According to history, as many as five million Christians were martyred during the reign of these emperors. The last emperor, Diocletian, was considered the worst antagonist of Christianity.

It has been said that the blood of martyrs is the seed of the church. Because the apostolic church lost its first love, it lost its ministry and power. The church that followed was the church of persecution.

When the church was persecuted by Saul of Tarsus, her faith and prayers, which were for the conversion of her mortal enemy, brought peace to the churches. When Peter was thrown into prison and condemned to death, God's people prayed, and an angel came and set him free. (See Acts 12:3–10.) Paul and Silas were thrown into prison at Philippi, but they prayed and sang praises, and God sent an earthquake to free them. (See Acts 16:23–26.) Evidently, those in this church age did not have that kind of faith. Nevertheless, they endured, and the "overcomers" were promised not to be hurt of the second death. (See Revelation 2:11.)

PERGAMOS
REVELATION 2:12-17 IMPERIAL FAVOR

The church at Pergamos pictures the church of imperial favor from AD 312–476. Pergamos had been the capital of the Roman province of Asia for two centuries from 133 BC. It was an important city that had one of the largest libraries in the world at that time. The library contained twenty thousand scrolls—an immense number in an age when every scroll had to be copied by hand. Our word *parchment* is derived from *pergamis,* a kind of writing material on which the New Testament was written. This material was invented in the city of Pergamos.

Pergamos was the ancient center of world learning. It was also the center of the worship of Aesculapius, the god of healing. Aesculapius was called *Zoter,* meaning "savior." The emblem of this god was the serpent. Sufferers were allowed to spend the night in the temple while tame and harmless snakes glided over the floor. Pergamos was also the center of Caesar

REVELATION 2

¹²And to the angel of the church in Pergamos write; These things says He which has the sharp sword with two edges;

¹³I know your works, and where you dwell, even where Satan's seat is: and you hold fast My name, and have not denied My faith, even in those days wherein Antipas was My faithful martyr, who was slain among you, where Satan dwell.

¹⁴But I have a few things against you, because you have there them that hold the doctrine of Balaam, who taught Balak to cast a stumbling block before the children of Israel, to eat things sacrificed to idols, and to commit fornication.

¹⁵So have you also them that hold the doctrine of the Nicolaitanes, which thing I hate.

¹⁶Repent; or else I will come to you quickly, and will fight against them with the sword of My mouth.

¹⁷He that has an ear, let him hear what the Spirit says to the churches; To him that overcomes will I give to eat of the hidden manna, and will give him a white stone, and in the stone a new name written, which no man knows saving he that receives it.

———————————————

———————————————

———————————————

———————————————

worship and the worship of many Greek idols. Today, Pergamos is no longer a city.

Jesus *commended* this church:

I know your works, and where you dwell, even where Satan's seat is: and you hold fast My name, and have not denied My faith, even in those days wherein Antipas was My faithful martyr, who was slain among you, where Satan dwell.
(Revelation 2:13)

Jesus *condemned* this church:

But I have a few things against you, because you have there them that hold the doctrine of Balaam, who taught Balak to cast a stumbling block before the children of Israel, to eat things sacrificed to idols, and to commit fornication. So have you also them that hold the doctrine of the Nicolaitans, which thing I hate.
(Revelation 2:14–15)

Jesus *counseled* this church:

Repent; or else I will come to you quickly, and will fight against them with the sword of My mouth. (Revelation 2:16)

Jesus *challenged* this church:

He that has an ear, let him hear what the Spirit says to the churches; To him that overcomes will I give to eat of the hidden manna, and will give him a white stone, and in the stone a new name written, which no man knows saving he that receives it. (Revelation 2:17)

For over two centuries, the church had endured much persecution. Satan had tried to destroy Christianity by imprisonment, death, and sword. The final persecution under Diocletian was horrendous; he burned Christians at the stake or boiled them in oil. But the devil's efforts failed—Christianity eventually became the state religion.

The change to imperial favor happened in a very unique way. Constantine, general of the Roman army, was having difficulties, and one day—according to his account—he saw in the sky the vision of the Cross and the words, "By this conquer." He did conquer, and the next year, when he became emperor of Rome, he made Christianity the state religion. It was thus protected by the empire. That, however, proved to be a compromising situation, which is always negative and never positive. Constantine took pagan temples and made them into church buildings. Pagan rituals and Christian practices were combined. It ended up a curse and not a blessing. When the church was elevated to acceptance, it lost its power and its blessing.

The name *Pergamos* means "married." This church was united with the world.

Pergamos was considered "Satan's seat" (see Revelation 2:13), because Satan thought he was ruling the Christian kingdom. It was also where the cult of "emperer worship" began.

Christ spoke of the doctrine of Balaam (see Revelation 2:14)—who certainly was a compromiser.

The *"doctrine of the Nicolaitans"* (Revelation 2:15) means "to conquer the laity." They would be conquered by a false clergy who would consider themselves unquestionable, and the headship of Christ would be ignored. The church thus became more Roman than Christian. Christ spoke of using *"the sword of My mouth"* (Revelation 2:16) to deal with this condition.

In AD 410, Alaric captured and sacked the city of Rome. Thus, the imperial court there no longer had

REVELATION 2

[18]And to the angel of the church in Thyatira write; These things says the Son of God, who has His eyes like to a flame of fire, and His feet are like fine brass;

[19]I know your works, and charity, and service, and faith, and your patience, and your works; and the last to be more than the first.

[20]Notwithstanding I have a few things against you, because you permit that woman Jezebel, which calls herself a prophetess, to teach and to seduce My servants to commit fornication, and to eat things sacrificed to idols.

[21]And I gave her space to repent of her fornication; and she repented not.

[22]Behold, I will cast her into a bed, and them that commit adultery with her into great tribulation, except they repent of their deeds.

[23]And I will kill her children with death; and all the churches shall know that I am He which searches the reins and hearts: and I will give to every one of you according to your works.

[24]But to you I say, and to the rest in Thyatira, as many as have not this doctrine, and which have not known the depths of Satan, as they speak; I will put upon you no other burden.

[25]But that which you have already hold fast till I come.

favors to grant to the church or anyone else. Later, Attila, "the scourge of God," ravaged much of Italy and then marched on Rome but did not take Rome because Pope Leo entered into a contract with Attila in AD 451 and finally persuaded him to withdraw. When Odoacer (a German chieftan) took over Rome in AD 476, it marked the end of the Pergamos period.

THYATIRA
REVELATION 2:18-29 PAPACY

The church at Pergamos paved the way for the apostate and harlot church, the church at Thyatira—the papal church from around AD 450 onward. *Thyatira* means "a continual sacrifice." It produced much false doctrine.

The empire of Rome had fallen, making way for the dark ages, represented by the church of Thyatira and its prophetess, Jezebel. Thyatira did not have the *political* importance of other cities that have been mentioned. It was, however, a center that had *commercial* importance in Paul's day.

Lydia, seller of purple, came from Thyatira. (See Acts 16:14.) Plants that produced purple dye are still commercially grown in that area. Thyatira possessed many skilled trades. These presented Christians with a problem, because they were associated with the worship of heathen gods. The Christians ate meat that had been offered to idols, and drank wine that had been poured out as a libation to the gods. A woman whom Christ calls "Jezebel" was associated with these trades, and she urged Christians to compromise by joining them.

It was not emperor worship that was attacking the church at this time, but conformity to the world for material prosperity. How ironic that today only a small slum with narrow, dirty streets remains of this once great commercial city.

The name of Jezebel in Revelation 2:20 is taken from the Old Testament:

> *For it was so, when Jezebel cut off the prophets of the LORD, that Obadiah took a hundred prophets, and hid them by fifty in a cave, and fed them with bread and water…. Was it not told my lord what I did when Jezebel slew the prophets of the LORD, how I hid a hundred men of the LORD's prophets by fifty in a cave, and fed them with bread and water?* (1 Kings 18:4, 13)

> *And it came to pass, when Joram saw Jehu, that he said, Is it peace, Jehu? And he answered, What peace, so long as the whoredoms of your mother Jezebel and her witchcrafts are so many?* (2 Kings 9:22)

Another depiction of Jezebel is found in Revelation 17:

> *And upon her forehead was a name written, MYSTERY, BABYLON THE GREAT, THE MOTHER OF HARLOTS AND ABOMINATIONS OF THE EARTH. And I saw the woman drunken with the blood of the saints, and with the blood of the martyrs of Jesus: and when I saw her, I wondered with great admiration.* (Revelation 17:5–6)

The church of Thyatira had a lust for temporal power, but the overcomers of this church were promised to rule and reign with Christ:

> *And he that overcomes, and keeps My works to the end, to him will I give power over the nations: and he shall rule them with a rod of*

²⁶And he that overcomes, and keeps My works to the end, to him will I give power over the nations:

²⁷and he shall rule them with a rod of iron; as the vessels of a potter shall they be broken to shivers: even as I received of My Father.

²⁸And I will give him the morning star.

²⁹He that has an ear, let him hear what the Spirit says to the churches.

NOTES

_____
_____
_____
_____
_____
_____
_____
_____
_____
_____
_____
_____
_____
_____
_____
_____

iron; as the vessels of a potter shall they be broken to shivers: even as I received of My Father.
(Revelation 2:26–27)

Ask of Me, and I shall give You the heathen for Your inheritance, and the uttermost parts of the earth for your possession. You shall break them with a rod of iron; You shall dash them in pieces like a potter's vessel. (Psalm 2:8–9)

The church age represented by Thyatira was a time of great darkness. However, there were some outstanding Christians who came out of this period: John Wycliffe, John Huss, Savonarola, and others. There were many martyrs during this time.

Jesus *commended* this church:

I know your works, and charity, and service, and faith, and your patience, and your works; and the last to be more than the first.
(Revelation 2:19)

Jesus *condemned* this church:

Notwithstanding I have a few things against you, because you permit that woman Jezebel, which calls herself a prophetess, to teach and to seduce My servants to commit fornication, and to eat things sacrificed to idols. And I gave her space to repent of her fornication; and she repented not. Behold, I will cast her into a bed, and them that commit adultery with her into great tribulation, except they repent of their deeds. And I will kill her children with death; and all the churches shall know that I am He which searches the reins and hearts: and I will give to every one of you according to your works. (Revelation 2:20–23)

Jesus *counseled* this church:

But to you I say, and to the rest in Thyatira, as many as have not this doctrine, and which have not known the depths of Satan, as they speak; I will put upon you no other burden. But that which you have already hold fast till I come.
(Revelation 2:24–25)

Jesus *challenged* this church:

And he that overcomes, and keeps My works to the end, to him will I give power over the nations: and he shall rule them with a rod of iron; as the vessels of a potter shall they be broken to shivers: even as I received of My Father. And I will give him the morning star. (Revelation 2:26–28)

Remember, overcoming is accomplished through believing:

For whatsoever is born of God overcomes the world: and this is the victory that overcomes the world, even our faith. (1 John 5:4)

CHAPTER THREE

SARDIS

REVELATION 3:1-6 REFORMATION

Sardis, the church of the Reformation (AD 1517), in John's day, was about thirty miles southeast of Thyatira. At the center of a knot of five different highways, Sardis was a great and wealthy commercial center noted for its carpet industry. It was finally destroyed by an earthquake. Within the church, there were a few believers who remained strong and faithful.

Jesus *commended* this church:

And to the angel of the church in Sardis write; These things says He that has the seven Spirits of God, and the seven stars; I know your works, that you have a name that you live, and are dead. (Revelation 3:1)

Jesus *condemned* this church:

Be watchful, and strengthen the things which remain, that are ready to die: for I have not found your works perfect before God. (Revelation 3:2)

Jesus *counseled* this church:

REVELATION 3

¹And to the angel of the church in Sardis write; These things says He that has the seven Spirits of God, and the seven stars; I know your works, that you have a name that you live, and are dead.

²Be watchful, and strengthen the things which remain, that are ready to die: for I have not found your works perfect before God.

³Remember therefore how you have received and heard, and hold fast, and repent. If therefore you shall not watch, I will come on you as a thief, and you shall not know what hour I will come upon you.

⁴You have a few names even in Sardis which have not defiled their garments; and they shall walk with Me in white: for they are worthy.

⁵He that overcomes, the same shall be clothed in white raiment; and I will not blot out his name out of the book of life, but I will confess his name before My Father, and before His angels.

⁶He that has an ear, let him hear what the Spirit says to the churches.

NOTES

_____

_____

_____

_____

_____

_____

_____

_____

_____

_____

_____

_____

_____

_____

_____

_____

_____

_____

_____

_____

_____

_____

_____

_____

_____

_____

_____

_____

_____

Be watchful, and strengthen the things which remain, that are ready to die: for I have not found your works perfect before God. Remember therefore how you have received and heard, and hold fast, and repent. If therefore you shall not watch, I will come on you as a thief, and you shall not know what hour I will come upon you.

(Revelation 3:2, 3)

Jesus *challenged* this church:

You have a few names even in Sardis which have not defiled their garments; and they shall walk with Me in white: for they are worthy. He that overcomes, the same shall be clothed in white raiment; and I will not blot out his name out of the book of life, but I will confess his name before My Father, and before His angels. (Revelation 3:4, 5)

Sardis means "the escaping." It seemed, however, to lack the power and gifts of the Holy Spirit. The seven Spirits of God mentioned in Revelation 3:1 are not seven different Spirits, but seven phases of the operation of the Holy Spirit as mentioned in Isaiah 11:2:

1. The Spirit of the Lord

2. The Spirit of wisdom

3. The Spirit of understanding

4. The Spirit of counsel

5. The Spirit of might

6. The Spirit of knowledge

7. The Spirit of the fear of the Lord

The saints at Sardis did not have the activity of the power of the Holy Spirit, but Jesus said there were a few saints who had not defiled their garments. When we think of the reformers and martyrs—like George Fox, John Knox, Zwingli, Savanarola, and

John Huss—who lifted up their voices against these evils, our lives are deeply touched. They made the way for this church.

There is a story told about this city that I think you would enjoy. King Cyrus once captured the city. On Mount Tmolus, behind it, was the citadel of Sardis. Because it was so steep, the position seemed to be untouchable, but one of the Persian soldiers detected a Lydian sentinel climbing down to retrieve his helmet. The Persian carefully noted the path and marked it in his memory. That night he led a band of troops to the top of the battlements. The battlements were unguarded because no one thought an ememy could find their way up the mountain. That night, the fortress and Sardis were taken.

The same thing happened two centuries later under Antiochus. It is no wonder Jesus told the church at Sardis:

If therefore you shall not watch, I will come on you as a thief, and you shall not know what hour I will come upon you. (Revelation 3:3)

Twenty years after the birth of Jesus, Sardis was destroyed in an earthquake. Tiberius, the reigning emperor, remitted taxation for a period of five years, and the city was rebuilt. It was not a center of emperor worship, but it was notorious for immorality—loose living. It had ceased to watch, and its enemies had infiltrated.

Sardis was alive materially, but spiritually it was dead. Today, Sardis is the scene of ruin. No Christians, as far as we know, reside on this spot.

Christ's message to this church was that men must not compromise with sin; they must live righteously if they wish have a part in the Book of Life. (See Revelation 3:5.)

REVELATION 3

⁷And to the angel of the church in Philadelphia write; These things says He that is holy, He that is true, He that has the key of David, He that opens, and no man shuts; and shuts, and no man opens;

⁸I know your works: behold, I have set before you an open door, and no man can shut it: for you have a little strength, and have kept My word, and have not denied My name.

⁹Behold, I will make them of the synagogue of Satan, which say they are Jews, and are not, but do lie; behold, I will make them to come and worship before your feet, and to know that I have loved you.

¹⁰Because you have kept the word of My patience, I also will keep you from the hour of temptation, which shall come upon all the world, to try them that dwell upon the earth.

¹¹Behold, I come quickly: hold that fast which you have, that no man take your crown.

¹²Him that overcomes will I make a pillar in the temple of My God, and he shall go no more out: and I will write upon him the name of My God, and the name of the city of My God, which is new Jerusalem, which comes down out of heaven from My God: and I will write upon him My new name.

¹³He that has an ear, let him hear what the Spirit says to the churches.

PHILADELPHIA

REVELATION 3:7–13 LATTER-DAY OUTPOURING

Philadelphia means "brotherly love." In John's day, Philadelphia stood on a very important site. It bordered three cities: Lydia, Mysia, and Phrygia. It was, therefore, the gateway to the east and the center of Greek civilization in that part of the world. Philadelphia had been founded with the purpose of spreading the Greek language and culture—to make the "barbarians" more civilized. Christ encouraged the Christians at Philadelphia to take advantage of their geographical location to spread the gospel. He said, *"Behold, I have set before you an open door"* (verse 8).

What is the open door spoken of by Christ? Undoubtedly the open door speaks of the gospel. The Philadelphia church was the great missionary church:

> *But the angel of the Lord by night opened the prison doors, and brought them forth, and said, Go, stand and speak in the temple to the people all the words of this life.* (Acts 5:19–20)

> *For a great door and effectual is opened to me, and there are many adversaries.* (1 Corinthians 16:9)

> *Furthermore, when I came to Troas to preach Christ's gospel, and a door was opened to me of the Lord, I had no rest in my spirit, because I found not Titus my brother: but taking my leave of them, I went from there into Macedonia.* (2 Corinthians 2:12–13)

> *Meanwhile praying also for us, that God would open to us a door of utterance, to speak the mystery of Christ, for which I am also in bonds.* (Colossians 4:3)

The open door also refers to Christ:

Then said Jesus to them again, Verily, verily, I say to you, I am the door of the sheep. (John 10:7)

Behold, I stand at the door, and knock: if any man hear My voice, and open the door, I will come in to him, and will sup with him, and he with Me. (Revelation 3:20)

The open door could also refer to the rapture of the church; in chapter four we see a door open in heaven and John caught up into heaven. That could certainly typify the rapture of the church.

Jesus *commended* this church:

I know your works: behold, I have set before you an open door, and no man can shut it: for you have a little strength, and have kept My word, and have not denied My name. Behold, I will make them of the synagogue of Satan, which say they are Jews, and are not, but do lie; behold, I will make them to come and worship before your feet, and to know that I have loved you. Because you have kept the word of My patience, I also will keep you from the hour of temptation, which shall come upon all the world, to try them that dwell upon the earth. (Revelation 3:8–10)

Jesus had no *condemnation* for this church.

Jesus *counseled* this church:

Behold, I come quickly: hold that fast which you have, that no man take your crown. (Revelation 3:11)

Jesus *challenged* this church:

Him that overcomes will I make a pillar in the temple of My God, and he shall go no more out:

and I will write upon him the name of My God, and the name of the city of My God, which is new Jerusalem, which comes down out of heaven from My God: and I will write upon him My new name. (Revelation 3:12)

The earthquake that destroyed Sardis also damaged Philadelphia. The emperor of Rome helped them to rebuild. They were very grateful for the contribution and for the rebuilding of their shattered city. The name of the city was even changed to Neo-Caesarea—"The New Town of Caesar." In light of the earthquake and name change, it is easy to understand Christ's words in Revelation 3:12 concerning a pillar and a new name.

It was also the case that whenever a public official made a large contribution to the city, they would add a pillar to one of the temples and write his name on it.

When the Muslim religion spread, Philadelphia stood as one of the last Christian cities. The city still exists today in western Turkey under the name of Alasehir, which means "city of God." It has a population of about ten thousand. Interestingly, it is said that there is one pillar that still stands after almost 2,000 years!

Christ mentioned *"the key of David"* to the church at Philadelphia:

And to the angel of the church in Philadelphia write; These things says He that is holy, He that is true, He that has the key of David, He that opens, and no man shuts; and shuts, and no man opens. (Revelation 3:7)

This probably refers back to the keys mentioned in the first chapter:

I am He that lives, and was dead; and, behold, I am alive for evermore, Amen; and have the keys of hell and of death. (Revelation 1:18)

Jesus mentioned keys to Peter:

And I will give to you the keys of the kingdom of heaven: and whatsoever you shall bind on earth shall be bound in heaven: and whatsoever you shall loose on earth shall be loosed in heaven. (Matthew 16:19)

There are many promises to the house of David:

And I will clothe him with your robe, and strengthen him with your girdle, and I will commit your government into his hand: and he shall be a father to the inhabitants of Jerusalem, and to the house of Judah. And the key of the house of David will I lay upon his shoulder; so he shall open, and none shall shut; and he shall shut, and none shall open. (Isaiah 22:21–22)

There is a connection also between the keys of death and Hell and the key to the house of David from Peter's sermon:

For David speaks concerning Him, I foresaw the Lord always before my face, for He is on my right hand, that I should not be moved: therefore did my heart rejoice, and my tongue was glad; moreover also my flesh shall rest in hope…. Therefore being a prophet, and knowing that God had sworn with an oath to Him, that of the fruit of His loins, according to the flesh, He would raise up Christ to sit on His throne; He seeing this before spoke of the resurrection of Christ, that His soul was not left in hell, neither His flesh did see corruption. (Acts 2:25–26, 30–31)

REVELATION 3

¹⁴And to the angel of the church of the Laodiceans write; These things says the Amen, the faithful and true witness, the beginning of the creation of God;

¹⁵I know your works, that you are neither cold nor hot: I would you were cold or hot.

¹⁶So then because you are lukewarm, and neither cold nor hot, I will spew you out of My mouth.

¹⁷Because you say, I am rich, and increased with goods, and have need of nothing; and know not that you are wretched, and miserable, and poor, and blind, and naked:

¹⁸I counsel you to buy of Me gold tried in the fire, that you may be rich; and white raiment, that you may be clothed, and that the shame of your nakedness do not appear; and anoint your eyes with eye salve, that you may see.

¹⁹As many as I love, I rebuke and chasten: be zealous therefore, and repent.

²⁰Behold, I stand at the door, and knock: if any man hear My voice, and open the door, I will come in to him, and will sup with him, and he with Me.

²¹To him that overcomes will I grant to sit with Me in My throne, even as I also overcame, and am set down with My Father in His throne.

²²He that has an ear, let him hear what the Spirit says to the churches.

When Christ went down into hell, God gave Him the keys to hell. Consequently, He not only opened the gates, but He took with Him the righteous who were confined in that place, including David, the king. Now the promises of the Davidic covenant can be fulfilled. Christ is coming again, and He will occupy the throne of David. The faithful church will rule with Christ:

To him that overcomes will I grant to sit with Me in My throne, even as I also overcame, and am set down with My Father in His throne.
(Revelation 3:21)

The synagogue of Satan (see Revelation 3:9) were the Jews who had repeatedly rejected Jesus Christ.

Undoubtedly the Philadelphia church refers to the closing period of the church age (as does the Laodicean church). This is the church of evangelism of our day—the church that is looking for His return. It had kept its first love. They had spurned the doctrine of Balaam, the Nicolaitans, and Jezebel with her idolatry and her whoredoms.

This church will be kept from the hour of temptation or tribulation mentioned in Revelation 3:10. Christ spoke of this period of tribulation in Matthew 24.

LAODICEA
REVELATION 3:14-21 LAST-DAY INDIFFERENCE

Laodicea is the lukewarm church. Both Philadelphia and Laodicea are end-time churches. Laodicea does not come out of Philadelphia; it is contemporary with it. *Laodicea* means "people," and it was a church of lukewarm people.

Laodicea occupied a large, fertile area in the valley of Lycus. The city was founded in 250 BC by Antiochus II and named after his wife Laodice. It was damaged by the same earthquake that hurt Philadelphia and Sardis. Lots of sheep were raised in this area. Much of the residents' wealth came from the clothing industry, which exported garments to all parts of the world. Christ, therefore, counseled them to buy white raiment that they might be clothed and the shame of their nakedness not appear. (See Revelation 3:18.)

The Laodiceans were steeped in Greek culture. Notice how Christ describes Himself to this church:

> And to the angel of the church of the Laodiceans write; These things says the Amen, the faithful and true witness, the beginning of the creation of God.   (Revelation 3:14)

All you can know about God is found in Christ. He has the Spirit without measure, and all things were created by Him.

The Laodiceans worshipped the god of healing and prepared an ointment of nard to cure sore ears and sometimes eyes. They were also famous for an eye powder used in healing eyes. Thus we can see the significance of Christ's words to them, to *"anoint your eyes with eye salve, that you may see"* (Revelation 3:18).

Jesus had no *commendation* for this church. Jesus *condemned* this church:

> So then because you are lukewarm, and neither cold nor hot, I will spew you out of My mouth. Because you say, I am rich, and increased with goods, and have need of nothing; and know not that you are wretched, and miserable, and poor, and blind, and naked.

Jesus *counseled* this church:

I counsel you to buy of Me gold tried in the fire, that you may be rich; and white raiment, that you may be clothed, and that the shame of your nakedness do not appear; and anoint your eyes with eye salve, that you may see.
(Revelation 3:18)

Jesus *challenged* this church:

To him that overcomes will I grant to sit with Me in My throne, even as I also overcame, and am set down with My Father in His throne.
(Revelation 3:21)

Today, there is no city of Laodicea. Ephesus, Thyatira, and Laodicea are the only three churches of these seven that are mentioned outside of Revelation in the New Testament. Paul mentioned Laodicea in his New Testament letter to the Colossians:

For I would that you knew what great conflict I have for you, and for them at Laodicea, and for as many as have not seen my face in the flesh.
(Colossians 2:1)

Salute the brethren which are in Laodicea, and Nymphas, and the church which is in his house. And when this epistle is read among you, cause that it be read also in the church of the Laodiceans; and that you likewise read the epistle from Laodicea. (Colossians 4:15–16)

The Laodicean church of *our day* is a lukewarm church—partly hot and partly cold, self-satisfied, boastful, and empty. Christ calls to this church, stands at the door, and knocks:

Behold, I stand at the door, and knock: if any man hear My voice, and open the door, I will come in to him, and will sup with him, and he with Me. (Revelation 3:20)

We certainly see both aspects of the Laodicean church in our day: we have the cold, liberal churches and the hot, turned-on churches.

OVERVIEW OF SEVEN CHURCHES					
Church	Time	Commendation	Condemnation	Counsel	Challenge
Ephesus	Apostolic	Faithful in service; hate deeds of Nicolaitans	Left first love	Repent	Eat of Tree of Life
Smyrna	Persecution	Faithful in persecution; poor, but rich	None	Fear not; be faithful	Not hurt of second death
Pergamos	Imperial Favor	Did not deny the faith in spite of Satan	Doctrine of Nicolaitans; Balaam	Repent	Eat hidden manna; white stone; new name
Thyatira	Papacy	Good works, charity, service, faith, patience	Wicked woman Jezebel	Hold fast till I come	Power over nations; morning star
Sardis	Reformation	Faithful few are worthy	Dead works; not perfect	Be watchful hold fast; repent	White raiment; confessed before Father
Philadelphia	Present Day	Kept His Word; did not deny His name	None	Hold that fast which you have	Pillar in temple; new name
Laodicea	Present Day	None	Lukewarm; blind; naked	Buy of Me gold; anoint your eyes	Sit with Christ on throne

CHAPTER FOUR

In chapter four, we are entering into the next segment, or room, of the book of Revelation. We have completed the church ages; the first three chapters of Revelation dealt with the seven churches of prophecy. At the end of this age, the rapture takes place, as taught in the New Testament, especially in 1 Thessalonians 4:13–17 and 1 Corinthians 15:51, 52. The scene of chapter four takes place in heaven following the rapture.

Somewhere high in the heavens a throne is set: the throne of God. Paul knew of this third heaven. John was also caught up into it. Job spoke of this place:

He stretches out the north over the empty place,
and hangs the earth upon nothing.   (Job 26:7)

In chapters four and five, *throne* is referred to eighteen times; it is the focal point for the activities that follow.

The first words of the fourth chapter of Revelation indicate that these events happen *after* the church age:

After this I looked, and, behold, a door was opened in heaven: and the first voice which I heard was as it were of a trumpet talking with

REVELATION 4

¹After this I looked, and, behold, a door was opened in heaven: and the first voice which I heard was as it were of a trumpet talking with me; which said, Come up here, and I will show you things which must be hereafter.

²And immediately I was in the Spirit: and, behold, a throne was set in heaven, and One sat on the throne.

³And He that sat was to look upon like a jasper and a sardine stone: and there was a rainbow round about the throne, in sight like to an emerald.

⁴And round about the throne were four and twenty seats: and upon the seats I saw four and twenty elders sitting, clothed in white raiment; and they had on their heads crowns of gold.

⁵And out of the throne proceeded lightnings and thunderings and voices: and there were seven lamps of fire burning before the throne, which are the seven Spirits of God.

⁶And before the throne there was a sea of glass like to crystal: and in the midst of the throne, and round about the throne, were four beasts full of eyes before and behind.

⁷And the first beast was like a lion, and the second beast like a calf, and the third beast had a face as a man, and the fourth beast was like a flying eagle.

⁸And the four beasts had each of them six wings about him; and they were full of eyes inside: and they rest not day and night, saying, Holy, holy, holy, Lord God Almighty, which was, and is, and is to come.

⁹And when those beasts give glory and honor and thanks to Him that sat on the throne, who lives for ever and ever,

¹⁰the four and twenty elders fall down before Him that sat on the throne, and worship Him that lives for ever and ever, and cast their crowns before the throne, saying,

¹¹You are worthy, O Lord, to receive glory and honor and power: for You have created all things, and for Your pleasure they are and were created.

NOTES

_____

_____

_____

_____

_____

_____

_____

_____

_____

_____

_____

me; which said, Come up here, and I will show you things which must be hereafter.

(Revelation 4:1)

When we read about the Philadelphia church (which represents the present church age), a door was opened for them. (See Revelation 3:8.) Now, in chapter four, we read of a door opened in heaven. Christ promised that He would keep the Philadelphia church from the hour of temptation, the great tribulation. This door *"opened in heaven"* and the voice *"of a trumpet"* undoubtedly points to the rapture of the overcomers which keeps them from going through the tribulation. *Rapture* derives from a Latin word meaning "to take by force, take from danger to come, take in an atom of time, or claim for one's own."

Paul also mentioned a trumpet in relation to the rapture:

Behold, I show you a mystery; We shall not all sleep, but we shall all be changed, in a moment, in the twinkling of an eye, at the last trump: for the trumpet shall sound, and the dead shall be raised incorruptible, and we shall be changed.

(1 Corinthians 15:51, 52)

Paul mentioned a trumpet again in his letter to the Thessalonians:

For the Lord Himself shall descend from heaven with a shout, with the voice of the archangel, and with the trump of God: and the dead in Christ shall rise first. (1 Thessalonians 4:16)

The voice of the trumpet here in Revelation 4:1 said, *"Come up here."* This certainly speaks of the rapture. The same words, *"Come up here"* are spoken of the two witnesses:

And they heard a great voice from heaven saying to them, Come up here. And they ascended up to heaven in a cloud; and their enemies beheld them. (Revelation 11:12)

Enoch was a sign of the rapture. (See Genesis 5:24.) He was taken to heaven *before* the judgment of the flood, while Noah and his family were kept safe on top of the flood waters.

In chapter four, we are in heaven. Twenty-four elders (*elder* means "leader") are singing the song of the redeemed. They wear victors' crowns rather than *diadems* or kingly crowns.

Let's remember that John was not literally transported to heaven—he was caught up in the spirit, transported by vision.

John saw a judgment throne:

And immediately I was in the Spirit: and, behold, a throne was set in heaven, and One sat on the throne. (Revelation 4:2)

Daniel saw a similar vision:

I beheld till the thrones were cast down, and the Ancient of Days did sit, whose garment was white as snow, and the hair of His head like the pure wool: His throne was like the fiery flame, and His wheels as burning fire. (Daniel 7:9)

There is a rainbow around God's throne. (See Revelation 4:3). It is perfectly circular, showing God's eternal purpose and covenant with the earth. Although John sees the throne of judgment, the rainbow is present as a token of God's covenant with all flesh never to destroy the inhabitants of the world by a flood:

And I will establish My covenant with you; neither shall all flesh be cut off any more by the

_____

_____

_____

_____

_____

_____

_____

_____

_____

_____

_____

_____

_____

_____

_____

_____

_____

_____

_____

_____

_____

_____

_____

_____

_____

waters of a flood; neither shall there any more be a flood to destroy the earth…. And God said to Noah, This is the token of the covenant, which I have established between Me and all flesh that is upon the earth. (Genesis 9:11, 17)

The twenty-four elders of verse four represent the overcomers mentioned earlier in Revelation:

Him that overcomes will I make a pillar in the temple of My God, and he shall go no more out: and I will write upon him the name of My God, and the name of the city of My God, which is new Jerusalem, which comes down out of heaven from My God: and I will write upon him My new name. (Revelation 3:12)

They are a heavenly priesthood—twelve represent Israel and twelve represent the church. In the Old Testament, the priesthood was divided into twenty-four orders, or courses. (See 1 Chronicles 24:3–19.) There were twenty-four priests especially chosen out of a total number of twenty-four thousand. (See 1 Chronicles 23:4–23.) It could easily be that the twenty-four elders represent the twelve tribes of Israel and the twelve apostles of the Lamb.

The earth will be judged but will not come to a cataclysmic end. Lightning, voices, and thunders come forth from the throne. These are all signs of judgment. This was the same way God visited judgment on Egypt:

And Moses stretched forth his rod toward heaven: and the LORD sent thunder and hail, and the fire ran along upon the ground; and the LORD rained hail upon the land of Egypt. (Exodus 9:23)

When Israel sinned in asking the Lord for a king, God sent thunder:

*So Samuel called to the L*ORD*; and the L*ORD *sent thunder and rain that day: and all the people greatly feared the L*ORD *and Samuel.*
(1 Samuel 12:18)

People must be purged by blood (see Hebrews 9:19–22), but the earth must be purged by fire. This will be the *day of the Lord*:

But after your hardness and impenitent heart treasure up to yourself wrath against the day of wrath and revelation of the righteous judgment of God. (Romans 2:5)

But the day of the Lord will come as a thief in the night; in the which the heavens shall pass away with a great noise, and the elements shall melt with fervent heat, the earth also and the works that are therein shall be burned up.
(2 Peter 3:10)

The "day of Christ" is the *rapture* of the church:

That you be not soon shaken in mind, or be troubled, neither by spirit, nor by word, nor by letter as from us, as that the day of Christ is at hand. Let no man deceive you by any means: for that day shall not come, except there come a falling away first, and that man of sin be revealed, the son of perdition. (2 Thessalonians 2:2–3)

The "day of the Lord" is Armageddon:

Having your conversation honest among the Gentiles: that, whereas they speak against you as evildoers, they may by your good works, which

———————————
———————————
———————————
———————————
———————————
———————————
———————————
———————————
———————————
———————————
———————————
———————————
———————————
———————————
———————————
———————————
———————————
———————————
———————————
———————————
———————————
———————————
———————————
———————————
———————————
———————————
———————————

they shall behold, glorify God in the day of visitation. (1 Peter 2:12)

We will see judgment fire again and again:

And out of the throne proceeded lightnings and thunderings and voices: and there were seven lamps of fire burning before the throne, which are the seven Spirits of God. (Revelation 4:5)

The first angel sounded, and there followed hail and fire mingled with blood, and they were cast upon the earth: and the third part of trees was burned up, and all green grass was burned up. (Revelation 8:7)

And the third angel sounded, and there fell a great star from heaven, burning as it were a lamp, and it fell upon the third part of the rivers, and upon the fountains of waters. (Revelation 8:10)

And men were scorched with great heat, and blasphemed the name of God, which has power over these plagues: and they repented not to give Him glory. (Revelation 16:9)

Every one of the seven trumpet plagues carry fire.

There will be much activity in heaven by the twenty-four elders, by the living ones, beasts, horsemen, and angels. They are organized for God's work:

Let the saints be joyful in glory: let them sing aloud upon their beds. Let the high praises of God be in their mouth, and a twoedged sword in their hand; to execute vengeance upon the heathen, and punishments upon the people; to bind their kings with chains, and their nobles with fetters of iron; to execute upon them the judgment written: this honor have all His saints. Praise you the Lord. (Psalm 149:5–9)

Do you not know that the saints shall judge the world? and if the world shall be judged by you, are you unworthy to judge the smallest matters? (1 Corinthians 6:2)

One key thing to remember is that there is much singing and worship in heaven. Before every great event of redemption, there will be a great and grand praise service in heaven.

Let's look at the four beasts of Revelation 4:6–8:

This description of the four beasts is taken from the four-faced creature of Ezekiel:

As for the likeness of their faces, they four had the face of a man, and the face of a lion, on the right side: and they four had the face of an ox on the left side; they four also had the face of an eagle. (Ezekiel 1:10)

These beasts, or *"living creatures,"* as some translations have it, reflect the nature of God:

Beloved, now are we the sons of God, and it does not yet appear what we shall be: but we know that, when He shall appear, we shall be like Him; for we shall see Him as He is. (1 John 3:2)

Remember, there is much worship in the book of revelation. We are told in Revelation 4:9 that the living creatures *"give glory and honor and thanks to Him that sat on the throne."* The twenty-four elders also worship the Lord. This is the praise of the redeemed before the wrath that is to come.

The "Harmony of Revelation" on the next page will help you as we continue our study through chapter 16.

HEAVEN	EVENT	EARTH
	**HARMONY OF REVELATION** Chapters 4–11 and 12–16	
4:1–3	Rapture	12:1–5
4:4–11	Saints in heaven	
5:1–7	The seven-sealed book	
5:8–14	Saints sing the redemption song in heaven	
	Satan attempts to prevent the resurrection	12:3, 4
	War with Satan and his angels	12:7, 8
	Satan cast down to earth	12:9–12
	Satan persecutes the church left behind	12:13–17
	The universal power of the beast	13:1–8
	The satanic trinity	13:11–18
6:1–8	The four horsemen—gospel preached by agents from heaven amid judgments and plagues	14:6–20
6:9–11	Tribulation saints awaiting their resurrection	
6:12–17	Earthquakes and falling stars hinder Satan	12:15, 16
7:1–8	144,000 saved Israelites remain on earth	14:1–5
7:9–17	All tribulation saints raised	
8:1–5	Preparation for seven last plagues	15:1–8
8:7	1st trumpet vial—the earth	16:1, 2
8:8, 9	2nd trumpet vial—the sea	16:3
8:10, 11	3rd trumpet vial—the rivers	16:4–7
8:12, 13	4th trumpet vial—the sun	16:8, 9
9:1–12	5th trumpet vial—the seat of the beast	16:10, 11
9:13–21	6th trumpet vial—the river Euphrates	16:12
10:1–11	Christ takes legal possession of the earth	
	Satan counters by marshalling his forces	16:13–16
11:1–13	The two witnesses and their message	16:15
11:15–19	7th trumpet vial—the return of Christ	16:17–21

Reprinted by permission from *All Things New* by Arthur Bloomfield; published and copyright 1971, Bethany House Publishers, Minneapolis, Minnesota 55438.

CHAPTER FIVE

Man lost dominion over the earth when Adam fell. The book in the right hand of God in this chapter is evidently the title deed of the earth:

And I saw in the right hand of Him that sat on the throne a book written inside and on the backside, sealed with seven seals. (verse 1)

This title deed to the earth was given to Adam by God, but Adam lost it to Satan through sin. As long as his book is sealed, Satan is in control of the earth.

A good picture of this matter of the title deed is found in the book of Jeremiah. According to Jeremiah 25:11–14, Jeremiah knew that the captivity of Israel would continue for seventy years; God revealed it to him. But Jeremiah also believed that God would restore the nation. As evidence of his faith, Jeremiah purchased a field that was his by right of inheritance:

So Hanameel my uncle's son came to me in the court of the prison according to the word of the Lord, *and said to me, Buy my field, I pray you, that is in Anathoth, which is in the country of Benjamin: for the right of inheritance is yours, and the redemption is yours; buy it for*

REVELATION 5

[1]And I saw in the right hand of Him that sat on the throne a book written inside and on the backside, sealed with seven seals.

[2]And I saw a strong angel proclaiming with a loud voice, who is worthy to open the book, and to loose the seals thereof?

[3]And no man in heaven, nor in earth, neither under the earth, was able to open the book, neither to look thereon.

[4]And I wept much, because no man was found worthy to open and to read the book, neither to look thereon.

[5]And one of the elders says to me, Weep not: behold, the Lion of the tribe of Juda, the Root of David, has prevailed to open the book, and to loose the seven seals thereof.

[6]And I beheld, and, lo, in the midst of the throne and of the four beasts, and in the midst of the elders, stood a Lamb as it had been slain, having seven horns and seven eyes, which are the seven Spirits of God sent forth into all the earth.

[7]And He came and took the book out of the right hand of Him that sat upon the throne.

[8]And when He had taken the book, the four beasts and four and twenty elders fell down before the Lamb, having every one of them harps, and golden vials full of odors, which are the prayers of saints.

⁹And they sung a new song, saying, You are worthy to take the book, and to open the seals thereof: for You were slain, and have redeemed us to God by Your blood out of every kindred, and tongue, and people, and nation;

¹⁰and have made us to our God kings and priests: and we shall reign on the earth.

¹¹And I beheld, and I heard the voice of many angels round about the throne and the beasts and the elders: and the number of them was ten thousand times ten thousand, and thousands of thousands;

¹²saying with a loud voice, Worthy is the Lamb that was slain to receive power, and riches, and wisdom, and strength, and honor, and glory, and blessing.

¹³And every creature which is in heaven, and on the earth, and under the earth, and such as are in the sea, and all that are in them, heard I saying, Blessing, and honor, and glory, and power, be to Him that sits upon the throne, and to the Lamb for ever and ever.

¹⁴And the four beasts said, Amen. And the four and twenty elders fell down and worshiped Him that lives for ever and ever.

NOTES

_____

_____

_____

yourself. Then I knew that this was the word of the LORD. (Jeremiah 32:8)

Jeremiah had witnesses, and he put the evidence of the purchase in an earthen vessel and buried it:

Thus says the LORD of hosts, the God of Israel; Take these evidences, this evidence of the purchase, both which is sealed, and this evidence which is open; and put them in an earthen vessel, that they may continue many days. For thus says the LORD of hosts, the God of Israel; Houses and fields and vineyards shall be possessed again in this land. (verses 14–15)

Revelation 4 and 5 reveal that it is time for the rightful heirs to take the title deed of the earth back from Satan. The rightful heirs are those who have been raptured or resurrected, and they sing the song of redemption; they are anticipating the redemption of the earth.

Let's look again at redemption. Three things were lost in the garden:

1. Intimacy with God

But of the tree of the knowledge of good and evil, you shall not eat of it: for in the day that you eat thereof you shall surely die. (Genesis 2:17)

But of the tree of the knowledge of good and evil, you shall not eat of it: for in the day that you eat thereof you shall surely die. (Ezekiel 18:4)

2. Innocence

In the sweat of your face shall you eat bread, till you return to the ground; for out of it were you taken: for dust you are, and to dust shall you return. (Genesis 3:19)

3. Confidence

And to Adam He said, Because you have hearkened to the voice of your wife, and have eaten of the tree, of which I commanded you, saying, You shall not eat of it: cursed is the ground for your sake; in sorrow shall you eat of it all the days of your life; thorns also and thistles shall it bring forth to you; and you shall eat the herb of the field. (Genesis 3:17–18)

All three of these must return to the original owner for redemption to be complete.

The life, death, resurrection, ascension, and return of Jesus Christ affords *full* redemption:

1. Eternal Life

2. Resurrection

3. Ascension (rapture of the living and dead)

In Revelation 5:4, we read that John *"wept much,"* but Christ came upon the scene as the Kinsman Redeemer. (See Ruth 4:1–12.) Christ has a right to redeem us by reason of His incarnation. (Luke 1:30–35.) He became the near-Kinsman, and by reason of what He accomplished on the cross, He can ransom us. (See Matthew 20:28.)

There are four *books* related to redemption and regeneration mentioned in the Bible:

1. The Title Deed to the Earth:

And one of the elders says to me, Weep not: behold, the Lion of the tribe of Juda, the Root of David, has prevailed to open the book, and to loose the seven seals thereof. And I beheld, and, lo, in the midst of the throne and of the four beasts, and in the midst of the elders, stood a Lamb as it had been slain, having seven horns and seven eyes, which are the seven Spirits of

_____
_____
_____
_____
_____
_____
_____
_____
_____
_____
_____
_____
_____
_____
_____
_____
_____
_____
_____
_____
_____
_____
_____
_____
_____

God sent forth into all the earth. And He came and took the book out of the right hand of Him that sat upon the throne.   (Revelation 5:5–7)

2. The Book of Life:

A fiery stream issued and came forth from before Him: thousand thousands ministered to Him, and ten thousand times ten thousand stood before Him: the judgment was set, and the books were opened.   (Daniel 7:10)

3. The Book of Judgment:

And I saw the dead, small and great, stand before God; and the books were opened: and another book was opened, which is the book of life: and the dead were judged out of those things which were written in the books according to their works.   (Revelation 20:12)

4. The Book of Remembrance:

Then they that feared the Lord spoke often one to another: and the Lord hearkened, and heard it, and a book of remembrance was written before Him for them that feared the Lord, and that thought upon His name.   (Malachi 3:16)

The song of *redemption* in Revelation 5:9–10 is sung only by saints, because the angels are not *redeemed*. We are the ones returned to our original Owner by the blood of the Lord Jesus Christ, the Lamb of God.

According to verses 9 and 10, Jesus is worthy to open the scroll for three reasons:

1.   He was slain on the cross.

2.   He purchased all men with His blood.

3. He made them kings and priests.

It's important that we understand two laws: the law of *possession* and the law of *inheritance*. The law of inheritance is greater. Satan had the earth under the law of possession. This means it is only temporary. Soon it will go back to the rightful heirs:

> *The land shall not be sold for ever: for the land is Mine; for you are strangers and sojourners with Me. And in all the land of your possession you shall grant a redemption for the land. If your brother be waxed poor, and has sold away some of his possession, and if any of his kin come to redeem it, then shall he redeem that which his brother sold.* (Leviticus 25:23–25)

> *In whom you also trusted, after that you heard the word of truth, the gospel of your salvation: in whom also after that you believed, you were sealed with that holy Spirit of promise, which is the earnest of our inheritance until the redemption of the purchased possession, to the praise of His glory.* (Ephesians 1:13–14)

Chapters four and five introduce us to the events which signal the return of the earth back to the saints:

> *And the kingdom and dominion, and the greatness of the kingdom under the whole heaven, shall be given to the people of the saints of the Most High, whose kingdom is an everlasting kingdom, and all dominions shall serve and obey Him.* (Daniel 7:27)

Satan does not want to give up the earth. Therefore, as the seals are broken, violent forces begin to strike the earth. They come from heaven, they come from earth, and they come from evil spirits from

_____

_____

_____

_____

_____

_____

_____

_____

_____

_____

_____

_____

_____

_____

_____

_____

_____

_____

_____

_____

_____

_____

_____

beneath the earth. The full and final repossession of the earth is recorded in chapter 19.

Now we are ready to view the opening of the seven seals and to behold the events which will shortly come to pass!

CHAPTER SIX

Chapter six begins with the breaking of the seven seals. The breaking of each seal brings a tragedy on the earth. With the breaking of each seal, the redemption of the earth comes one step nearer.

Many people will be saved during the time of the first six seals: *"And this gospel of the kingdom shall be preached in all the world for a witness to all nations; and then shall the end come"* (Matthew 24:14).

The breaking of the first seal reveals the rider on the white horse; the Lion of the tribe of Judah is now ready to go forth to take over the earth and restore it to its rightful heirs. We are quite sure that this rider is Christ because *white* is connected with righteousness. Christ has *white* hair, the saints have *white* robes, God's judgment throne is *white*, and Christ says the overcomers in the church *"shall walk with Me in white"* (Revelation 3:4).

Christ is going forth to take vengeance; the bow symbolizes conquest:

REVELATION 6

¹And I saw when the Lamb opened one of the seals, and I heard, as it were the noise of thunder, one of the four beasts saying, Come and see.

²And I saw, and behold a white horse: and he that sat on him had a bow; and a crown was given to him: and he went forth conquering, and to conquer.

NOTES

_____

_____

_____

_____

_____

_____

_____

_____

_____

_____

_____

_____

_____

_____

Who raised up the righteous man from the east, called him to His foot, gave the nations before him, and made him rule over kings? He gave them as the dust to his sword, and as driven stubble to his bow. (Isaiah 41:2)

God judges the righteous, and God is angry with the wicked every day. If he turn not, He will whet His sword; He has bent His bow, and made it ready. (Psalm 7:11–12)

He has bent His bow like an enemy: He stood with His right hand as an adversary, and slew all that were pleasant to the eye in the tabernacle of the daughter of Zion: He poured out His fury like fire. (Lamentations 2:4)

Your bow was made quite naked, according to the oaths of the tribes, even your word. Selah. You did cleave the earth with rivers. (Habakkuk 3:9)

Revelation 6:2 says that *"a crown was given"* to the rider on the white horse. Let's look at two kinds of *crowns*:

1. The Victor's Crown

2. The Crown of Righteousness

When Christ goes forth *"to conquer,"* the Greek word *iko* is used, which means "to prevail; to get the victory":

Nay, in all these things we are more than conquerors through Him that loved us. (Romans 8:37)

Christ is absolutely the Conqueror, and He is coming to conquer the earth:

These things I have spoken to you, that in Me you might have peace. In the world you shall have tribulation: but be of good cheer; I have overcome the world. (John 16:33)

To him that overcomes will I grant to sit with Me in My throne, even as I also overcame, and am set down with My Father in His throne. (Revelation 3:21)

And I saw, and behold a white horse: and he that sat on him had a bow; and a crown was given to him: and he went forth conquering, and to conquer. (Revelation 6:2)

Upon the opening of the second seal, we see a red horse and its rider who takes peace from the earth. Many believe this will be a third world war:

And when these things begin to come to pass, then look up, and lift up your heads; for your redemption draws near. (Luke 21:28)

We know that chaos will break out in the world during this time, and in the midst of it, the Antichrist will begin to rise in power.

Following the war, we see the black horse of famine. The symbolism of this third seal is brought out by Jeremiah:

REVELATION 6

³And when He had opened the second seal, I heard the second beast say, Come and see.

⁴And there went out another horse that was red: and power was given to him that sat thereon to take peace from the earth, and that they should kill one another: and there was given to him a great sword.

⁵And when He had opened the third seal, I heard the third beast say, Come and see. And I beheld, and lo a black horse; and he that sat on him had a pair of balances in his hand.

⁶And I heard a voice in the midst of the four beasts say, A measure of wheat for a penny, and three measures of barley for a penny; and see you hurt not the oil and the wine.

NOTES

_____

_____

_____

_____

_____

_____

_____

_____

_____

REVELATION 6

⁷And when He had opened the fourth seal, I heard the voice of the fourth beast say, Come and see.

⁸And I looked, and behold a pale horse: and his name that sat on him was Death, and Hell followed with him. And power was given to them over the fourth part of the earth, to kill with sword, and with hunger, and with death, and with the beasts of the earth.

⁹And when He had opened the fifth seal, I saw under the altar the souls of them that were slain for the word of God, and for the testimony which they held:

¹⁰and they cried with a loud voice, saying, How long, O Lord, holy and true, do You not judge and avenge our blood on them that dwell on the earth?

¹¹And white robes were given to every one of them; and it was said to them, that they should rest yet for a little season, until their fellow-servants also and their brethren, that should be killed as they were, should be fulfilled.

NOTES

_____

_____

_____

_____

The word of the LORD that came to Jeremiah concerning the dearth. Judah mourns, and the gates thereof languish; they are black to the ground; and the cry of Jerusalem is gone up.

(Jeremiah 14:1–2)

Our skin was black like an oven because of the terrible famine. (Lamentations 5:10)

When the nations of the world have mobilized for war, there are none left behind to raise the crops. When the third horseman says, *"see you hurt not the oil and the wine,"* he is limiting the effects of famine so that it doesn't go to the extreme.

As the fourth seal is opened, the pale horse of death kills *"with sword, and with hunger, and with death, and with the beasts of the earth"* (verse 8). The beasts here could easily be the beasts of Revelation 13:1, 11. They destroy without mercy. The tremendous slaughter seems to take place in the area of the old Roman empire. Many will die, and many will be swallowed up in Hades. This will be a time of tribulation on the earth for the Christians, but a time of relative peace for the Jews.

After the work of these four horsemen is described, the fifth seal is opened, which reveals the result of what has been happening up to this point: the killing of some saints by the Antichrist. The curtain is pulled back in heaven, and we see the tribulation martyrs receiving their white robes. The bloody persecution they experienced came straight from the Antichrist on the earth.

The reason there are martyred *tribulation* saints is that Satan is infuriated with the previous rapture of the church. Consequently, he comes against those who were saved during the tribulation. The tribulation martyrs are slain for the Word of God and the testimony that they hold; Satan takes vengeance on those who have a testimony for Jesus, who oppose his false claims, and who expose his hideous character.

In chapter seven, we will see the rapture of the remaining tribulation saints, which infuriates Satan even more.

Please note that people are *conscious* after death. Here in the fifth seal, we see the *activity* of the souls who were martyred. We are reminded of Paul's words to the Corinthians:

We are confident, I say, and willing rather to be absent from the body, and to be present with the Lord. (2 Corinthians 5:8)

We enter now a transition period from the time of tribulation for the saints to the great and terrible day of the Lord—the time of God's wrath on the wicked, unbelieving world. Compare the sixth seal of Revelation 6:12–15 to Luke 21:25–26:

REVELATION 6

¹²And I beheld when He had opened the sixth seal, and, lo, there was a great earthquake; and the sun became black as sackcloth of hair, and the moon became as blood;

¹³and the stars of heaven fell to the earth, even as a fig tree casts her untimely figs, when she is shaken of a mighty wind.

¹⁴And the heaven departed as a scroll when it is rolled together; and every mountain and island were moved out of their places.

¹⁵And the kings of the earth, and the great men, and the rich men, and the chief captains, and the mighty men, and every bondman, and every free man, hid themselves in the dens and in the rocks of the mountains;

¹⁶and said to the mountains and rocks, Fall on us, and hide us from the face of Him that sits on the throne, and from the wrath of the Lamb:

¹⁷for the great day of His wrath is come; and who shall be able to stand?

NOTES

_____

_____

_____

_____

_____

And I beheld when He had opened the sixth seal, and, lo, there was a great earthquake; and the sun became black as sackcloth of hair, and the moon became as blood; and the stars of heaven fell to the earth, even as a fig tree casts her untimely figs, when she is shaken of a mighty wind. And the heaven departed as a scroll when it is rolled together; and every mountain and island were moved out of their places. And the kings of the earth, and the great men, and the rich men, and the chief captains, and the mighty men, and every bondman, and every free man, hid themselves in the dens and in the rocks of the mountains.

(Revelation 6:12–15)

And there shall be signs in the sun, and in the moon, and in the stars; and upon the earth distress of nations, with perplexity; the sea and the waves roaring; men's hearts failing them for fear, and for looking after those things which are coming on the earth: for the powers of heaven shall be shaken.

(Luke 21:25–26)

In the sixth seal, we have the vision of Christ before the great and terrible day of the Lord:

And said to the mountains and rocks, Fall on us, and hide us from the face of Him that sits on the

throne, and from the wrath of the Lamb: for the
great day of His wrath is come; and who shall be
able to stand? (Revelation 6:16–17)

This *"great day of His wrath"* is spoken of in many
Old Testament prophecies:

The great day of the Lord is near, it is near, and
hastes greatly, even the voice of the day of the
Lord: the mighty man shall cry there bitterly.
That day is a day of wrath, a day of trouble and
distress, a day of wasteness and desolation, a day
of darkness and gloominess, a day of clouds and
thick darkness, a day of the trumpet and alarm
against the fenced cities, and against the high
towers. And I will bring distress upon men, that
they shall walk like blind men, because they have
sinned against the Lord: and their blood shall be
poured out as dust, and their flesh as the dung.
Neither their silver nor their gold shall be able
to deliver them in the day of the Lord's wrath;
but the whole land shall be devoured by the fire
of His jealousy: for He shall make even a speedy
riddance of all them that dwell in the land.
(Zephaniah 1:14–18)

By comparing Matthew 24:29–31 with Revelation
6:12–17 (the sixth seal), we will see that at this point
in Revelation, we are at the end of the first half of the
tribulation and at the beginning of the day of God's
wrath:

1. The sun and moon are darkened—this is the
   end of the tribulation:

_____
_____
_____
_____
_____
_____
_____
_____
_____
_____
_____
_____
_____
_____
_____
_____
_____
_____
_____
_____
_____
_____
_____

Immediately after the tribulation of those days shall the sun be darkened, and the moon shall not give her light, and the stars shall fall from heaven, and the powers of the heavens shall be shaken.

(Matthew 24:29)

And I beheld when He had opened the sixth seal, and, lo, there was a great earthquake; and the sun became black as sackcloth of hair, and the moon became as blood.

(Revelation 6:12)

2.   The stars of heaven fall:

Immediately after the tribulation of those days shall the sun be darkened, and the moon shall not give her light, and the stars shall fall from heaven, and the powers of the heavens shall be shaken.

(Matthew 24:29)

And the stars of heaven fell to the earth, even as a fig tree casts her untimely figs, when she is shaken of a mighty wind.

(Revelation 6:13)

3.   The sign of the Son of man appears in the heavens:

And then shall appear the sign of the Son of man in heaven: and then shall all the tribes of the earth mourn, and they shall see the Son of man coming in the clouds of heaven with power and great glory.

(Matthew 24:30)

And the heaven departed as a scroll when it is rolled together; and every mountain and island were moved out of their places.

(Revelation 6:14)

4. All the world sees the appearance of Christ:

And then shall appear the sign of the Son of man in heaven: and then shall all the tribes of the earth mourn, and they shall see the Son of man coming in the clouds of heaven with power and great glory.
(Matthew 24:30)

And said to the mountains and rocks, Fall on us, and hide us from the face of Him that sits on the throne, and from the wrath of the Lamb.
(Revelation 6:16)

5. There is great fear on earth:

And then shall appear the sign of the Son of man in heaven: and then shall all the tribes of the earth mourn, and they shall see the Son of man coming in the clouds of heaven with power and great glory.
(Matthew 24:30)

And the kings of the earth, and the great men, and the rich men, and the chief captains, and the mighty men, and every bondman, and every free man, hid themselves in the dens and in the rocks of the mountains; and said to the mountains and rocks, Fall on us, and hide us from the face of Him that sits on the throne, and from the wrath of the Lamb.
(Revelation 6:15–16)

6. Christ's elect will be gathered:

_____
_____
_____
_____
_____
_____
_____
_____
_____
_____
_____
_____
_____
_____
_____
_____
_____
_____
_____
_____
_____
_____
_____
_____
_____
_____

And He shall send His angels with a great sound of a trumpet, and they shall gather together His elect from the four winds, from one end of heaven to the other.
(Matthew 24:31)

After this I beheld, and, lo, a great multitude, which no man could number, of all nations, and kindreds, and people, and tongues, stood before the throne, and before the Lamb, clothed with white robes, and palms in their hands. And he said to me, These are they which came out of great tribulation, and have washed their robes, and made them white in the blood of the Lamb.
(Revelation 7:9, 14)

(This is the large rapture at the end of the first three-and-a-half years of the Tribulation.)

7.   Great wrath follows, along with judgment:

For as in the days that were before the flood they were eating and drinking, marrying and giving in marriage, until the day that Noah entered into the ark, and knew not until the flood came, and took them all away; so shall also the coming of the Son of man be.
(Matthew 24:38–39)

And said to the mountains and rocks, Fall on us, and hide us from the face of Him that sits on the throne, and from the wrath of the Lamb: for the great day of His wrath is come; and who shall be able to stand?
(Revelation 6:16–17)

The forces of nature will be used against Satan. The sun will be affected again at the sounding of the fourth trumpet:

And the fourth angel sounded, and the third part of the sun was smitten, and the third part of the moon, and the third part of the stars; so as the third part of them was darkened, and the day shone not for a third part of it, and the night likewise. (Revelation 8:12)

The sun, moon, and stars are darkened for one third of the day and night. During the fifth trumpet, the sun is darkened by the smoke of the locusts coming out of the bottomless pit.

Following these judgments, we see Christ on His throne. Men will be so frightened that they will seek holes in the rocks for refuge. Judgment will hit those who have hurt God's people:

Fear, and the pit, and the snare, are upon you, O inhabitant of the earth. And it shall come to pass, that he who flees from the noise of the fear shall fall into the pit; and he that comes up out of the midst of the pit shall be taken in the snare: for the windows from on high are open, and the foundations of the earth do shake. The earth is utterly broken down, the earth is clean dissolved, the earth is moved exceedingly. The earth shall reel to and fro like a drunkard, and shall be removed like a cottage; and the transgression thereof shall be heavy upon it; and it shall fall, and not rise again. And it shall come to pass in that day, that the Lord *shall punish the host of the high ones that are on high, and the kings of the earth upon the earth. And they shall be gathered together, as prisoners are gathered in the pit, and shall be shut up in the prison, and after many days shall they* be visited. *Then the moon shall be confounded, and the sun ashamed, when the* LORD *of hosts shall reign in mount Zion, and in Jerusalem, and before His ancients gloriously.* (Isaiah 24:17–23)

As in the days before the Exodus, God's judgments fall on the wicked, while His people are kept safe. In the next chapter, we will see God's people sealed as a means of protection against the dreadful sting of demon locusts that are loosed at the sounding of the fifth trumpet in Revelation 9.

SHOULD I BE CONCERNED WITH THE ANTICHRIST?

It is very important that we remain aware of the times we live in. Because of the signs we read about in Mathew 24, and then again in Revelation, it is very possible that the Antichrist is alive right now, in our time. This is not the time to go to sleep. All you have to do is look in the Bible for examples of people who fell asleep at the wrong time. Samson fell asleep on Delilah's lap and she cut off his hair and he lost his power and anointing. (See Judges 16:4–30.) Eli was sleeping when God was speaking to Samuel. (See 1 Samuel 3.) Sometimes, as Christians, we can be so busy trying to make a living and getting by that we fall asleep. In Acts, a man fell asleep while Paul was preaching and fell to his death out of a window! Fortunately, Paul prayed and he revived. (See Acts 20:9–10.) We need to wake up to the spiritual time in which we live. This is a time to remain alert to what the enemy is doing. It is a time to be aggressive in our faith.

EIGHT SIGNS OF THE ANTICHRIST

The Bible has warning signs for the Antichrist from Genesis through Revelation. We know the Antichrist will be like the devil, who steals, kills, and destroys, but there are eight signs by which we can recognize him.

1. HIS MOUTH

"…eyes like the eyes of man, and a mouth speaking great things."　　　　(Daniel 7:8)

And in the latter time of their kingdom, when the transgressors are come to the full, a king of fierce countenance, and understanding dark sentences, shall stand up.
　　　　　　　　　　　　　　　　　　　　　　　　　　　　(Daniel 8:23)

The Antichrist will speak beautiful, *"dark sentences"* that will draw people in like never before. That was one of the things about Hitler; he had a persuasive way of speaking. He mesmerized huge crowds with his speeches. Undoubtedly, he was obsessed, oppressed, and possessed by Satan, because never before has one man used his words to lead other people to commit such horrible murders and atrocities. The Antichrist will be like that.

2. HIS EYES

Part of the *"fierce countenance"* of the Antichrist will be his unusual eyes. When we look back in history at so many fallen leaders, despots who did terrible things in the world, you can almost see it in their eyes. You think, *Man, that is like the devil looking at me.*

3. RAISES TAXES

That's right. Daniel 11:20 says, *"Then shall stand up in his estate a raiser of taxes in the glory of the kingdom."* He will impose taxes, especially in Israel, and he will impose tremendous pressure on them.

4. PART JEWISH

The Antichrist will be Jewish (or part Jewish). He will put himself in a position to go into Israel, rebuild the temple with the Holy of Holies, and set an image of himself. The Jews would never accept someone to do this who is not Jewish.

5. PROSPERITY

He will raise taxes and then he will open arenas for jobs, making him quite popular for a period of time. *"Through his policy also he shall cause craft to prosper in his hand; and he shall magnify himself in his heart"* (Daniel 8:25).

6. WAR AND PEACE

The ten horns out of this kingdom are ten kings that shall arise: and another shall rise after them; and he shall be diverse from the first, and he shall subdue three kings.

(Daniel 7:24)

And the ten horns which you saw are ten kings, which have received no kingdom as yet; but receive power as kings one hour with the beast. These have one mind, and shall give their power and strength to the beast.... For God has put in their hearts to fulfill His will, and to agree, and give their kingdom to the beast. (Revelation 17:12–13, 17)

The ascent of the Antichrist will be fueled by war. The Antichrist is pictured with seven heads and ten horns. The seven heads are the seven ancient world empires that conquered and will dominate the Israelites—Egypt, Assyria, Babylon, Medo-Persia, Greece, Rome, and the Antichrist. The ten horns symbolize the ten nations lying within the borders of these ancient empires that will fall under the Antichrist's rule. In the beginning, he will conquer three countries, which will scare seven other countries to join his confederacy. He will curry Israel's favor by offering to make peace with her neighboring nations. Israel will then enter into a seven-year covenant with him.

7. EMULATES CHRIST

And I saw one of his heads as it were wounded to death; and his deadly wound was healed: and all the world wondered after the beast. (Revelation 13:3)

While the Antichrist holds the world's attention and the devotion of Israel, Satan will try to prove the Antichrist is the messiah. In an imitation of Christ, the Antichrist is killed, and because the people refuse to bury him, the world will see him rise from the dead.

8. WORSHIPPED

And they worshipped the dragon which gave power to the beast: and they worshipped the beast, saying, Who is like to the beast? who is able to make war with him? (Revelation 13:4)

Satan will give the Antichrist new powers to do lying signs and wonders, causing people to revere and worship him. Many people will believe he is god and follow his lead as he persecutes the remnant church.

HIS ULTIMATE END

We know that one of best outcomes of the battle of Armageddon is that the Antichrist and false prophet are thrown into the Lake of Fire to be persecuted forever. Satan is chained in the bottomless pit and his demons are expelled from the earth. (See Isaiah 24:21–22; Matthew 13:41–43; Revelation 19:20–21; 20:1–3.) Christ then takes possession of the earth and walks in victory through the eastern gate of His capital city, Jerusalem. His thousand-year reign of the world has begun.

WHAT CAN WE DO IN THE MEANTIME?

As His church, we have no alternative but to lean heavily on the Holy Spirit. In Romans 8:26, the Bible says that when we don't know what we should pray, the Spirit intercedes for us, to help us in our weakness. The Spirit will search your heart and reveal the will of God for your life in this time of waiting until the glorious appearing of Jesus Christ. Then, two verses later, we are reminded that *"all things work together for good to them that love God, to them who are the called according to His purpose"* (Romans 8:28).

When we pray in the Spirit, it makes all things work together for good—even when the world seems to be falling apart and the spirit of Antichrist is everywhere and people are backsliding and acting as if the Bible is not real. Even with the rise of persecution and false religious systems, when we pray in the Spirit, the Spirit praying within us is strengthening us for this time, as He continues to make all things work together for good.

SUMMARY OF SEALS 1-6

SEAL 1
Christ | White Horse | Conquest
Rev. 6:1–2

SEAL 4
Pale Horse | Death
Rev. 6:7–8

SEAL 2
Red Horse | War
Rev. 6:3–4

SEAL 5
Martyrs
Rev. 6:9–11

SEAL 3
Black Horse | Famine
Rev. 6:5–6

SEAL 6
Catastrophes on Earth
Rev. 6:12–17

CHAPTER SEVEN

Remember the purpose of the plagues: they strike hard at Satan and his kingdom—both spiritual and material. They also serve to hurt the earth, because cleansing will be essential in redemption. We will see that there is no difference between the trumpet judgments and the vial judgments except the viewpoint. The trumpet judgments are from a heavenly viewpoint; the vial judgments are from an earthly viewpoint.

Remember also that chapters 4–11 have to do with the heavenly viewpoint; the earthly viewpoint is given in chapters 12–16. There is really only a difference in the way it is presented. When we look from heaven, we see everything in chronological order, but when we look from earth, we see a topical presentation using many symbols.

God is going to send His wrath upon the earth and upon the ungodly, but God will send mercy upon His people; He seals the 144,000 before the opening of the seventh seal.

God's people are afforded protection in His time of judgment, just as Lot was protected from the destruction of Sodom and Gomorrah:

REVELATION 7

[1]And after these things I saw four angels standing on the four corners of the earth, holding the four winds of the earth, that the wind should not blow on the earth, nor on the sea, nor on any tree.

[2]And I saw another angel ascending from the east, having the seal of the living God: and he cried with a loud voice to the four angels, to whom it was given to hurt the earth and the sea,

[3]saying, Hurt not the earth, neither the sea, nor the trees, till we have sealed the servants of our God in their foreheads.

[4]And I heard the number of them which were sealed: and there were sealed a hundred and forty and four thousand of all the tribes of the children of Israel.

[5]Of the tribe of Juda were sealed twelve thousand. Of the tribe of Reuben were sealed twelve thousand. Of the tribe of Gad were sealed twelve thousand.

[6]Of the tribe of Aser were sealed twelve thousand. Of the tribe of Nepthalim were sealed twelve thousand. Of the tribe of Manasses were sealed twelve thousand.

[7]Of the tribe of Simeon were sealed twelve thousand. Of the tribe of Levi were sealed twelve thousand. Of the tribe of Issachar were sealed twelve thousand.

[8]Of the tribe of Zabulon were sealed twelve thousand. Of the

tribe of Joseph were sealed twelve thousand. Of the tribe of Benjamin were sealed twelve thousand.

⁹After this I beheld, and, lo, a great multitude, which no man could number, of all nations, and kindreds, and people, and tongues, stood before the throne, and before the Lamb, clothed with white robes, and palms in their hands;

¹⁰and cried with a loud voice, saying, Salvation to our God which sits upon the throne, and to the Lamb.

¹¹And all the angels stood round about the throne, and about the elders and the four beasts, and fell before the throne on their faces, and worshiped God,

¹²saying, Amen: blessing, and glory, and wisdom, and thanksgiving, and honor, and power, and might, be to our God for ever and ever. Amen.

¹³And one of the elders answered, saying to me, What are these which are arrayed in white robes? and from where came they?

¹⁴And I said to him, Sir, you know. And he said to me, These are they which came out of great tribulation, and have washed their robes, and made them white in the blood of the Lamb.

¹⁵Therefore are they before the throne of God, and serve Him day and night in His temple: and He that sits on the throne shall dwell among them.

Likewise also as it was in the days of Lot; they did eat, they drank, they bought, they sold, they planted, they built; but the same day that Lot went out of Sodom it rained fire and brimstone from heaven, and destroyed them all.
(Luke 17:28–29)

Haste you, escape there; for I cannot do any thing till you be come there. Therefore the name of the city was called Zoar. (Genesis 19:22)

Come, my people, enter you into your chambers, and shut your doors about you: hide yourself as it were for a little moment, until the indignation be overpast. For, behold, the LORD comes out of His place to punish the inhabitants of the earth for their iniquity: the earth also shall disclose her blood, and shall no more cover her slain.
(Isaiah 26:20–21)

In Revelation 7:1–4, we see the sealing of the 144,000. I believe these are literal Israelites. We do know that there will be a unifying of the two tribes with the ten tribes in the end-times, as recorded in Ezekiel 37:15–28.

THE TWELVE TRIBES

Revelation 7:5–8

TRIBE	MEANING
Judah	Praise
Ruben	Behold, a son
Gad	Troop
Asher	Happy
Naphtali	Wrestle
Manasseh	Cause to forget
Simeon	Hearing

TRIBE	MEANING
Levi	Attachment
Issachar	Reward
Zebulun	Abode
Joseph	May He add
Benjamin	Son of the right hand

Please note that Dan and Ephraim are not included in the sealing. God gave a warning in Deuteronomy that has a bearing on this:

Lest there should be among you man, or woman, or family, or tribe, whose heart turns away this day from the LORD your God to go and serve the gods of these nations; lest there should be among you a root that bears gall and wormwood; and it come to pass, when he hears the words of this curse, that he bless himself in his heart, saying, I shall have peace, though I walk in the imagination of my heart, to add drunkenness to thirst: the LORD will not spare him, but then the anger of the LORD and His jealousy shall smoke against that man, and all the curses that are written in this book shall lie upon him, and the LORD shall blot out his name from under heaven.
(Deuteronomy 29:18–20)

Both of these tribes were involved in the golden calf worship:

And he set the one in Bethel, and the other put he in Dan. And this thing became a sin: for the people went to worship before the one, even to Dan. (1 Kings 12:29–30)

However, they will have their allotted territory in the millennium:

¹⁶They shall hunger no more, neither thirst any more; neither shall the sun light on them, nor any heat.

¹⁷For the Lamb which is in the midst of the throne shall feed them, and shall lead them to living fountains of waters: and God shall wipe away all tears from their eyes.

NOTES

Now these are the names of the tribes. From the north end to the coast of the way of Hethlon, as one goes to Hamath, Hazarenan, the border of Damascus northward, to the coast of Hamath; for these are his sides east and west; a portion for Dan…. And by the border of Manasseh, from the east side to the west side, a portion for Ephraim. (Ezekiel 48:1, 5)

Before the great and terrible day begins and the seventh seal is broken, and before the seven trumpet angels can sound their trumpets, another angel comes for the sealing of the servants of God in their foreheads. God has a mark that protects those who love Him:

And the Lord said to him, Go through the midst of the city, through the midst of Jerusalem, and set a mark upon the foreheads of the men that sigh and that cry for all the abominations that be done in the midst thereof. (Ezekiel 9:4)

And they shall see His face; and His name shall be in their foreheads. (Revelation 22:4)

All of God's servants will have His name on their foreheads. It will be visible at the time of judgment to provide protection. It will be visible to the locust demons of chapter nine:

And it was commanded them that they should not hurt the grass of the earth, neither any green thing, neither any tree; but only those men which have not the seal of God in their foreheads. (Revelation 9:4)

This is just like the sign of the blood on the lintels of the doors of the Israelites in Egypt at the time of the Passover: it kept the destroying angel from entering their houses.

The seal could be the outpouring of the Holy Spirit:

And Jesus, when He was baptized, went up immediately out of the water: and, lo, the heavens were opened to Him, and he saw the Spirit of God descending like a dove, and lighting upon Him. (Matthew 3:16)

Labor not for the meat which perishes, but for that meat which endures to everlasting life, which the Son of man shall give to you: for Him has God the Father sealed. (John 6:27)

In whom you also trusted, after that you heard the word of truth, the gospel of your salvation: in whom also after that you believed, you were sealed with that holy Spirit of promise. (Ephesians 1:13)

The Antichrist will try to emulate God's mark with a mark of his own:

And he causes all, both small and great, rich and poor, free and bond, to receive a mark in their right hand, or in their foreheads: and that no man might buy or sell, save he that had the mark, or the name of the beast, or the number of his name. (Revelation 13:16–17)

Of course, the mark of the beast will not bring safety; it will bring disaster to those who take it:

And the third angel followed them, saying with a loud voice, If any man worship the beast and his image, and receive his mark in his forehead, or in his hand, the same shall drink of the wine

_____

_____

_____

_____

_____

_____

_____

_____

_____

_____

_____

_____

_____

_____

_____

_____

_____

_____

_____

_____

_____

_____

_____

_____

_____

_____

of the wrath of God, which is poured out without mixture into the cup of His indignation; and he shall be tormented with fire and brimstone in the presence of the holy angels, and in the presence of the Lamb. (Revelation 14:9–10)

There will be a great multitude of tribulation saints. (See Revelation 7:9, 14.) Many will be martyred; John saw them depicted in the fifth seal in chapter six. They are called God's elect:

Immediately after the tribulation of those days shall the sun be darkened, and the moon shall not give her light, and the stars shall fall from heaven, and the powers of the heavens shall be shaken: and then shall appear the sign of the Son of man in heaven: and then shall all the tribes of the earth mourn, and they shall see the Son of man coming in the clouds of heaven with power and great glory. And He shall send His angels with a great sound of a trumpet, and they shall gather together His elect from the four winds, from one end of heaven to the other.
(Matthew 24:29–31)

And shall not God avenge His own elect, which cry day and night to Him, though He bear long with them? I tell you that He will avenge them speedily. Nevertheless when the Son of Man comes, shall He find faith on the earth?
(Luke 18:7–8)

And they cried with a loud voice, saying, How long, O Lord, holy and true, do You not judge and avenge our blood on them that dwell on the earth? (Revelation 6:10)

These *"elect"* are not the highest order of the redeemed, but they are given palms and white robes as the firstfruits unto God. In the fifth seal, they were called the *"fellow-servants"* (Revelation 6:11).

CHAPTER EIGHT

The first six seals describe, in part, events during the first three-and-a-half years of the tribulation. The sixth seal speaks of heavenly phenomena (compare Acts 2:19–21), which leads into the seventh seal—the day of the Lord. The plagues are coming, and they are sent to harass and defeat the devil.

At this time, we will begin to see what Peter was talking about when he said the elements would melt with a fervent heat. The plagues contain the fire that Peter mentions. The seventh seal marks the beginning of the fire:

For this they willingly are ignorant of, that by the word of God the heavens were of old, and the earth standing out of the water and in the water: whereby the world that then was, being overflowed with water, perished: but the heavens and the earth, which are now, by the same word are kept in store, reserved to fire against the day of judgment and perdition of ungodly men. But, beloved, be not ignorant of this one thing, that one day is with the Lord as a thousand years, and a thousand years as one day. The Lord is not slack concerning His promise, as some men count

REVELATION 8

¹And when He had opened the seventh seal, there was silence in heaven about the space of half an hour.

²And I saw the seven angels which stood before God; and to them were given seven trumpets.

³And another angel came and stood at the altar, having a golden censer; and there was given to him much incense, that he should offer it with the prayers of all saints upon the golden altar which was before the throne.

⁴And the smoke of the incense, which came with the prayers of the saints, ascended up before God out of the angel's hand.

⁵And the angel took the censer, and filled it with fire of the altar, and cast it into the earth: and there were voices, and thunderings, and lightnings, and an earthquake.

⁶And the seven angels which had the seven trumpets prepared themselves to sound.

NOTES

_____

_____

_____

_____

_____

_____

_____

slackness; but is long-suffering to us-ward, not willing that any should perish, but that all should come to repentance. But the day of the Lord will come as a thief in the night; in the which the heavens shall pass away with a great noise, and the elements shall melt with fervent heat, the earth also and the works that are therein shall be burned up. Seeing then that all these things shall be dissolved, what manner of persons ought you to be in all holy conversation and godliness. (2 Peter 3:5–11)

When Peter wrote that the earth *"perished,"* he didn't mean that the earth totally vanished. The earth was purged by water; it will be purged again with fire. People are purged by blood; the physical earth will be purged by fire. Remember, all of the last seven plagues have fire. When the millennium arrives, there will be a time of reconstruction. It will take a thousand years to restore the earth to perfection:

And He that sat upon the throne said, Behold, I make all things new. And He said to me, Write: for these words are true and faithful.

(Revelation 21:5)

At the opening of the seventh seal, there is silence in heaven. This silence could be a memorial to the saints who have prayed and labored through the years. It is also *the calm before the storm*—now the time of Jacob's trouble has come:

Alas! for that day is great, so that none is like it: it is even the time of Jacob's trouble; but he shall be saved out of it. (Jeremiah 30:7)

The earthquake that accompanies the opening of the seventh seal will be a severe one:

For thus says the LORD of hosts; Yet once, it is a little while, and I will shake the heavens, and the earth, and the sea, and the dry land; and I will shake all nations, and the desire of all nations shall come: and I will fill this house with glory, says the LORD of hosts. (Haggai 2:6–7)

Earthquakes often accompany important events—at the giving of the law, for example:

And mount Sinai was altogether on a smoke, because the LORD descended upon it in fire: and the smoke thereof ascended as the smoke of a furnace, and the whole mount quaked greatly. (Exodus 19:18)

There was an earthquake at the time of Christ's death:

Jesus, when He had cried again with a loud voice, yielded up the ghost. And, behold, the veil of the temple was rent in two from the top to the bottom; and the earth did quake, and the rocks rent. (Matthew 27:50–51)

Hebrews 12:26–27 refers to the prophecy of Haggai and its judgments. This is the shaking. Now things happen in the heavens, for the sun is darkened and the moon is turned into blood. The first three-and-a-half years of the tribulation ends, and the great and terrible day of the Lord begins:

Immediately after the tribulation of those days shall the sun be darkened, and the moon shall not give her light, and the stars shall fall from heaven, and the powers of the heavens shall be shaken. (Matthew 24:29)

_____

_____

_____

_____

_____

_____

_____

_____

_____

_____

_____

_____

_____

_____

_____

_____

_____

_____

_____

_____

_____

_____

_____

_____

_____

_____

_____

And I will show wonders in heaven above, and signs in the earth beneath; blood, and fire, and vapor of smoke: the sun shall be turned into darkness, and the moon into blood, before that great and notable day of the Lord come.

(Acts 2:19–20)

Seven angels are given trumpets. Trumpets have always been used in the Bible to signal special occasions:

And the Lord shall be seen over them, and His arrow shall go forth as the lightning: and the Lord God shall blow the trumpet, and shall go with whirlwinds of the south. (Zechariah 9:14)

A trumpet will be blown at the rapture:

In a moment, in the twinkling of an eye, at the last trump: for the trumpet shall sound, and the dead shall be raised incorruptible, and we shall be changed. (1 Corinthians 15:52)

For the Lord Himself shall descend from heaven with a shout, with the voice of the archangel, and with the trump of God: and the dead in Christ shall rise first. (1 Thessalonians 4:16)

A trumpet will be blown at the day of the Lord:

Blow you the trumpet in Zion, and sound an alarm in my holy mountain: let all the inhabitants of the land tremble: for the day of the Lord comes, for it is near at hand. (Joel 2:1)

The great day of the Lord is near, it is near, and hastes greatly, even the voice of the day of the Lord: the mighty man shall cry there bitterly…. A day of the trumpet and alarm against the

fenced cities, and against the high towers.
                                    (Zephaniah 1:14, 16)

*And in that day there shall be a root of Jesse,
which shall stand for an ensign of the people; to it
shall the Gentiles seek: and His rest shall be glorious. And it shall come to pass in that day, that
the LORD shall set His hand again the second time
to recover the remnant of His people, which shall
be left, from Assyria, and from Egypt, and from
Pathos, and from Cush, and from Elam, and
from Shinar, and from Hamath, and from the
islands of the sea. And He shall set up an ensign
for the nations, and shall assemble the outcasts of
Israel, and gather together the dispersed of Judah
from the four corners of the earth.*
(Isaiah 11:10–12)

At the sounding of these trumpets in the book of
Revelation, the cities of the nations shall fall just as
the city of Jericho fell at the sound of trumpets:

*So the people shouted when the priests blew with
the trumpets: and it came to pass, when the
people heard the sound of the trumpet, and the
people shouted with a great shout, that the wall
fell down flat, so that the people went up into
the city, every man straight before him, and they
took the city.*   (Joshua 6:20)

The prayers mentioned in Revelation 8:3 are
prayers kept by God for perhaps as long as two thousand years. The censer is filled with fire in verse five;
there is vengeance in it. When the prayers of the saints
are answered, when they hit the earth, we read what
occurs:

REVELATION 8

⁷The first angel sounded, and there followed hail and fire mingled with blood, and they were cast upon the earth: and the third part of trees was burned up, and all green grass was burned up.

NOTES

_____

_____

_____

_____

_____

_____

_____

_____

_____

_____

_____

_____

_____

_____

_____

_____

_____

And the angel took the censer, and filled it with fire of the altar, and cast it into the earth: and there were voices, and thunderings, and lightnings, and an earthquake.   (Revelation 8:5)

Let's look at the progression of the seven trumpet plagues:

1

There is bad news for earth at the sounding of the first trumpet. (See Revelation 8:7.) As a result of hail mingled with fire, a third of the trees burn up and all green grass is burned. The greatest intensity of these judgments will be upon the territory of the beast in the Mediterranean area.

Five of the plagues of Egypt occur again in Revelation. This first plague with fire is similar to the hail that fell on the Egyptians:

And the LORD said to Moses, Stretch forth your hand toward heaven, that there may be hail in all the land of Egypt, upon man, and upon beast, and upon every herb of the field, throughout the land of Egypt. And Moses stretched forth his rod toward heaven: and the LORD sent thunder and hail, and the fire ran along upon the ground; and the LORD rained hail upon the land of Egypt. So there was hail, and fire mingled with the hail, very grievous, such as there was none like it in all the land of Egypt since it became a nation.
(Exodus 9:22–24)

God also sent fire and brimstone on Sodom and Gomorrah:

Then the LORD rained upon Sodom and upon Gomorrah brimstone and fire from the LORD out of heaven.   (Genesis 19:24)

2

The second trumpet judgment is like a flaming meteorite striking the earth. It causes a third part of the sea, a third of the sea animals, and a third of the ships to be destroyed. This is similar to the Nile turning to blood:

And Moses and Aaron did so, as the Lord *commanded; and he lifted up the rod, and smote the waters that were in the river, in the sight of Pharaoh, and in the sight of his servants; and all the waters that were in the river were turned to blood.* (Exodus 7:20)

3

The third trumpet judgment is similar to the second trumpet judgment except it affects the *land* rather than the sea. It causes a third part of the rivers and fresh waters on the land to be made bitter or poisonous. A meteorite evidently falls and impacts a third of the earth's rivers. The meteorite and its vapor impart something poisonous to the water of one of the rivers.

People die from drinking this poisonous water. *Wormwood* is named after a poisonous herb called *absinthe*. Jeremiah prophesied of God's judgment as wormwood:

Therefore thus says the Lord *of hosts, the God of Israel; Behold, I will feed them, even this people, with wormwood, and give them water of gall to drink.* (Jeremiah 9:15)

4

The fourth trumpet judgment causes the third part of the sun, moon, and stars to be smitten. On the fourth day of creation, God made the light, and with

REVELATION 8

⁸And the second angel sounded, and as it were a great mountain burning with fire was cast into the sea: and the third part of the sea became blood;

⁹and the third part of the creatures which were in the sea, and had life, died; and the third part of the ships were destroyed.

¹⁰And the third angel sounded, and there fell a great star from heaven, burning as it were a lamp, and it fell upon the third part of the rivers, and upon the fountains of waters;

¹¹and the name of the star is called Wormwood: and the third part of the waters became wormwood; and many men died of the waters, because they were made bitter.

¹²And the fourth angel sounded, and the third part of the sun was smitten, and the third part of the moon, and the third part of the stars; so as the third part of them was darkened, and the day shone not for a third part of it, and the night likewise.

¹³And I beheld, and heard an angel flying through the midst of heaven, saying with a loud voice, Woe, woe, woe, to the inhabiters of the earth by reason of the other voices of the trumpet of the three angels, which are yet to sound!

the fourth trumpet judgment, He will diminish the lights by one third (sixteen hours of darkness; eight hours of light). The age is ending, and darkness is settling over the earth; the illuminators of the night are affected.

One quarter of the day was darkened when Christ died:

> *Now from the sixth hour there was darkness over all the land to the ninth hour.*
>
> (Matthew 27:45)

In Revelation 8:13, we read of the warning angel before the sounding of the fifth trumpet judgment. The fifth, sixth, and seventh trumpet judgments are called *woes* because of their severity. The word *angel* in this verse is rendered *eagle* in some versions:

> *But they that wait upon the* Lord *shall renew their strength; they shall mount up with wings as eagles; they shall run, and not be weary; and they shall walk, and not faint.* (Isaiah 40:31)

> *Wherefore if they shall say to you, Behold, He is in the desert; go not forth: behold, He is in the secret chambers; believe it not. For as the lightning comes out of the east, and shines even to the west; so shall also the coming of the Son of man be. For wheresoever the carcass is, there will the eagles be gathered together.*
>
> (Matthew 24:26–28)

This eagle represents the activities of the saints during this time.

The first four trumpets are directed toward the earth, the sea, the rivers, and the sun. These judgments are caused by inanimate forces: heat, blood, fire, wormwood, and darkness. The last three trumpet judgments will be directed toward people—especially the kingdom of the beast.

These last three trumpet judgments are plagues brought by living beings: one comes from the bottomless pit; one comes from the river Euphrates; and one comes from heaven.

These "living" plagues are more terrible than the inanimate plagues. The fifth and sixth plagues will strike at men, and the seventh plague will *destroy them which destroy the earth* (Revelation 11:18).

These trumpets make sounds in heaven, but as earth looks up, they appear as vials poured out on them—there is no sound heard by those on earth. We will look more closely at the parallel between the trumpet and vial judgments when we come to chapter 16.

CHAPTER NINE

There is no question about *star wars* in heaven! God used the stars to defeat a heathen general:

They fought from heaven; the stars in their courses fought against Sisera. (Judges 5:20)

The wise men were guided by a star:

Saying, Where is He that is born King of the Jews? for we have seen His star in the east, and are come to worship Him. (Matthew 2:2)

Peter spoke of Jesus as the *"day star"*:

We have also a more sure word of prophecy; whereto you do well that you take heed, as to a light that shines in a dark place, until the day dawn, and the day star arise in your hearts. (2 Peter 1:19)

Jesus called Himself the *"Morning Star"*:

I Jesus have sent My angel to testify to you these things in the churches. I am the Root and the Offspring of David, and the Bright and Morning Star. (Revelation 22:16)

REVELATION 9

¹And the fifth angel sounded, and I saw a star fall from heaven to the earth: and to him was given the key of the bottomless pit.

²And he opened the bottomless pit; and there arose a smoke out of the pit, as the smoke of a great furnace; and the sun and the air were darkened by reason of the smoke of the pit.

³And there came out of the smoke locusts upon the earth: and to them was given power, as the scorpions of the earth have power.

⁴And it was commanded them that they should not hurt the grass of the earth, neither any green thing, neither any tree; but only those men which have not the seal of God in their foreheads.

⁵And to them it was given that they should not kill them, but that they should be tormented five months: and their torment was as the torment of a scorpion, when he strikes a man.

⁶And in those days shall men seek death, and shall not find it; and shall desire to die, and death shall flee from them.

⁷And the shapes of the locusts were like to horses prepared to battle; and on their heads were as it were crowns like gold, and their faces were as the faces of men.

⁸And they had hair as the hair of women, and their teeth were as the teeth of lions.

⁹And they had breastplates, as it were breastplates of iron; and the sound of their wings was as the sound of chariots of many horses running to battle.

¹⁰And they had tails like to scorpions, and there were stings in their tails: and their power was to hurt men five months.

¹¹And they had a king over them, which is the angel of the bottomless pit, whose name in the Hebrew tongue is Abaddon, but in the Greek tongue has his name Apollyon.

¹²One woe is past; and, behold, there come two woes more hereafter.

NOTES

The star that falls at the beginning of this chapter is Satan:

And the fifth angel sounded, and I saw a star fall from heaven to the earth: and to him was given the key of the bottomless pit. (Revelation 9:1)

Jesus pictured Satan's fall:

And He said to them, I beheld Satan as lightning fall from heaven. (Luke 10:18)

Stars in the book of Revelation symbolize different things; they can be human beings:

And He had in His right hand seven stars: and out of His mouth went a sharp two edged sword: and His countenance was as the sun shines in His strength…. The mystery of the seven stars which you saw in My right hand, and the seven golden candlesticks. The seven stars are the angels of the seven churches: and the seven candlesticks which you saw are the seven churches. (Revelation 1:16, 20)

And they that be wise shall shine as the brightness of the firmament; and they that turn many to righteousness as the stars for ever and ever. (Daniel 12:3)

They can be good angels or bad angels:

They fought from heaven; the stars in their courses fought against Sisera. (Judges 5:20)

And his tail drew the third part of the stars of heaven, and did cast them to the earth: and the dragon stood before the woman which was ready to be delivered, for to devour her child as soon as it was born. (Revelation 12:4)

They can be meteorites:

And the stars of heaven fell to the earth, even as a fig tree casts her untimely figs, when she is shaken of a mighty wind. (Revelation 6:13)

They can be the fixed stars of the sky:

And they that be wise shall shine as the brightness of the firmament; and they that turn many to righteousness as the stars for ever and ever. (Daniel 12:3)

For the stars of heaven and the constellations thereof shall not give their light: the sun shall be darkened in its going forth, and the moon shall not cause her light to shine. (Isaiah 13:10)

5

The fifth trumpet judgment comes against the beast and his kingdom. Remember, this is the first of three *"woes."* The angel takes the key and opens the bottomless pit, and the occupants come forth. They are hideous, supernatural locusts—kind of an infernal, angelic cherubim. They are a combination of man, lion, scorpion, and horse, and they have battle armor. They have some intelligence because they know not to hurt those who have the seal of God on their foreheads. Men do not die from the pain of the locusts' sting, but they desire to die because their stings cause such torment.

These locusts are demon spirits. They come out of the bottomless pit, which is where demons are kept. The bottomless pit is different from the lake of fire; the bottomless pit is a temporary prison. Demons didn't want Christ to send them there:

And when He went forth to land, there met Him out of the city a certain man, which had devils

———————————
———————————
———————————
———————————
———————————
———————————
———————————
———————————
———————————
———————————
———————————
———————————
———————————
———————————
———————————
———————————
———————————
———————————
———————————
———————————
———————————
———————————
———————————

long time, and ware no clothes, neither abode in any house, but in the tombs. When he saw Jesus, he cried out, and fell down before Him, and with a loud voice said, What have I to do with You, Jesus, You Son of God Most High? I beseech You, torment me not. (For He had commanded the unclean spirit to come out of the man. For oftentimes it had caught him: and he was kept bound with chains and in fetters; and he broke the bands, and was driven of the devil into the wilderness.) And Jesus asked him, saying, What is your name? And he said, Legion: because many devils were entered into him. And they besought Him that He would not command them to go out into the deep. (Luke 8:27–31)

The beast of Revelation 17 comes out of the bottomless pit:

The beast that you saw was, and is not; and shall ascend out of the bottomless pit, and go into perdition: and they that dwell on the earth shall wonder, whose names were not written in the book of life from the foundation of the world, when they behold the beast that was, and is not, and yet is. (Revelation 17:8)

Fallen angels are also kept in the bottomless pit:

And they had a king over them, which is the angel of the bottomless pit, whose name in the Hebrew tongue is Abaddon, but in the Greek tongue has his name Apollyon.

(Revelation 9:11)

Satan himself is kept in the bottomless pit during the millennium:

And I saw an angel come down from heaven, having the key of the bottomless pit and a great chain in his hand. And he laid hold on the dragon, that old serpent, which is the Devil, and Satan, and bound him a thousand years, and cast him into the bottomless pit, and shut him up, and set a seal upon him, that he should deceive the nations no more, till the thousand years should be fulfilled: and after that he must be loosed a little season. (Revelation 20:1–3)

This fifth trumpet judgment continues for five months (see Revelation 9:10), which is the same length of time as the flood (see Genesis 7:24) and about the length of time that natural locusts appear (May through September). The first four trumpets probably lasted only a few days each.

Who is the king of these demon locusts? We know he has two names: *Abaddon* in Hebrew, and *Apollyon* in Greek, which means "the destroyer." It is Satan, of course, and he has many ranks of angels under him. He seems to have authority over the bottomless pit at this time to let these demon spirits out. Eventually, we know that the key will be taken from him, and he will be thrown into the bottomless pit for a thousand years.

These locusts that Satan commands appear to be like those described in Joel chapters 1–2. Both prophecies speak of a day of darkness:

———————————
———————————
———————————
———————————
———————————
———————————
———————————
———————————
———————————
———————————
———————————
———————————
———————————
———————————
———————————
———————————
———————————
———————————
———————————
———————————
———————————
———————————

And the fourth angel sounded, and the third part of the sun was smitten, and the third part of the moon, and the third part of the stars; so as the third part of them was darkened, and the day shone not for a third part of it, and the night likewise.
(Revelation 8:12)

A day of darkness and of gloominess, a day of clouds and of thick darkness, as the morning spread upon the mountains: a great people and a strong; there has not been ever the like, neither shall be any more after it, even to the years of many generations. (Joel 2:2)

Both prophecies involve the blowing of a trumpet:

And the fifth angel sounded, and I saw a star fall from heaven to the earth: and to him was given the key of the bottomless pit.
(Revelation 9:1)

Blow you the trumpet in Zion, and sound an alarm in my holy mountain: let all the inhabitants of the land tremble: for the day of the LORD comes, for it is near at hand.
(Joel 2:1)

Both refer to locust-like creatures:

And there came out of the smoke locusts upon the earth: and to them was given power, as the scorpions of the earth have power.
(Revelation 9:3)

A fire devours before them; and behind them a flame burns: the land is as the garden of Eden before them, and behind them a desolate wilderness; yea, and nothing shall escape them. (Joel 2:3)

Both prophecies speak of creatures having power to injure but not to kill:

> And to them it was given that they should not kill them, but that they should be tormented five months: and their torment was as the torment of a scorpion, when he strikes a man.
> (Revelation 9:5)

> Before their face the people shall be much pained: all faces shall gather blackness.
> (Joel 2:6)

Both prophecies speak of creatures that are like horses:

> And the shapes of the locusts were like to horses prepared to battle; and on their heads were as it were crowns like gold, and their faces were as the faces of men.
> (Revelation 9:7)

> The appearance of them is as the appearance of horses; and as horsemen, so shall they run. (Joel 2:4)

Both prophecies liken the noise of the locusts' to the sound of chariots:

> And they had breastplates, as it were breastplates of iron; and the sound of their wings was as the sound of chariots of many horses running to battle.
> (Revelation 9:9)

> Like the noise of chariots on the tops of mountains shall they leap, like the noise of a flame of fire that devours the stubble, as a strong people set in battle array. (Joel 2:5)

REVELATION 9

¹³And the sixth angel sounded, and I heard a voice from the four horns of the golden altar which is before God,

¹⁴saying to the sixth angel which had the trumpet, Loose the four angels which are bound in the great river Euphrates.

¹⁵And the four angels were loosed, which were prepared for an hour, and a day, and a month, and a year, for to slay the third part of men.

¹⁶And the number of the army of the horsemen were two hundred thousand thousand: and I heard the number of them.

¹⁷And thus I saw the horses in the vision, and them that sat on them, having breastplates of fire, and of jacinth, and brimstone: and the heads of the horses were as the heads of lions; and out of their mouths issued fire and smoke and brimstone.

¹⁸By these three was the third part of men killed, by the fire, and by the smoke, and by the brimstone, which issued out of their mouths.

¹⁹For their power is in their mouth, and in their tails: for their tails were like serpents, and had heads, and with them they do hurt.

²⁰And the rest of the men which were not killed by these plagues yet repented not of the works of their hands, that they should not worship devils, and idols of gold, and silver, and brass, and stone, and of

Both of the armies show organization behind them:

And they had a king over them, which is the angel of the bottomless pit, whose name in the Hebrew tongue is Abaddon, but in the Greek tongue has his name Apollyon. (Revelation 9:11)	*They shall run like mighty men; they shall climb the wall like men of war; and they shall march every one on his ways, and they shall not break their ranks.* (Joel 2:7)

Both prophecies speak of spirit creatures:

And they had a king over them, which is the angel of the bottomless pit, whose name in the Hebrew tongue is Abaddon, but in the Greek tongue has his name Apollyon. (Revelation 9:11)	*Neither shall one thrust another; they shall walk every one in his path: and when they fall upon the sword, they shall not be wounded.* (Joel 2:8)

6

The sixth trumpet judgment is the second of the three woes and, of course, is a very severe judgment. A voice from the altar calls for vengeance rather than mercy. The four angels of Revelation 9:15 are evidently evil angels. Peter and Jude speak of these:

> *For if God spared not the angels that sinned, but cast them down to hell, and delivered them into chains of darkness, to be reserved to judgment.*
> (2 Peter 2:4)

And the angels which kept not their first estate, but left their own habitation, He has reserved in everlasting chains under darkness to the judgment of the great day. (Jude 6)

These four angels were bound in the river Euphrates. Why does the Euphrates have such significance?

Remember, the first attempts of the devil against humanity were in this area—this was where the garden of Eden was. The first murder was committed there. The apostasy, both before and after the flood, was there. This is the region where Israel had the most oppressive enemies. This is also the area where the Jews had their long captivity. It was here where oppressive world powers began. Thus, this area seems to be a center of Satan's evil.

The two hundred million horsemen mentioned in verse 16 are demonic spirits. These are evil spirits who kept not their first estate. They are to be judged in the day of the Lord:

And the angels which kept not their first estate, but left their own habitation, He has reserved in everlasting chains under darkness to the judgment of the great day. Even as Sodom and Gomorrha, and the cities about them in like manner, giving themselves over to fornication, and going after strange flesh, are set forth for an example, suffering the vengeance of eternal fire. (Jude 6–7)

For if God spared not the angels that sinned, but cast them down to hell, and delivered them into chains of darkness, to be reserved to judgment; and spared not the old world, but saved Noah the eighth person, a preacher of righteousness,

wood: which neither can see, nor hear, nor walk:

21neither repented they of their murders, nor of their sorceries, nor of their fornication, nor of their thefts.

NOTES

_____

_____

_____

_____

_____

_____

_____

_____

_____

_____

_____

_____

_____

_____

_____

_____

_____

_____

bringing in the flood upon the world of the ungodly.   (2 Peter 2:4–5)

For Christ also has once suffered for sins, the just for the unjust, that He might bring us to God, being put to death in the flesh, but quickened by the Spirit: by which also He went and preached to the spirits in prison; which sometime were disobedient, when once the long-suffering of God waited in the days of Noah, while the ark was a preparing, wherein few, that is, eight souls were saved by water.   (1 Peter 3:18–20)

And it came to pass, when men began to multiply on the face of the earth, and daughters were born to them, that the sons of God saw the daughters of men that they were fair; and they took them wives of all which they chose. And the Lord *said, My Spirit shall not always strive with man, for that he also is flesh: yet his days shall be a hundred and twenty years. There were giants in the earth in those days; and also after that, when the sons of God came in to the daughters of men, and they bore children to them, the same became mighty men which were of old, men of renown.*
(Genesis 6:1–4)

They, of course, belong to Satan's kingdom. Jesus preached to these spirits in prison:

By which also He went and preached to the spirits in prison; which sometime were disobedient, when once the long-suffering of God waited in the days of Noah, while the ark was a preparing, wherein few, that is, eight souls were saved by water.   (1 Peter 3:19–20)

Undoubtedly, these are angels who cohabited with the daughters of men. Their seed were called *nephilim*, which means "fallen ones." There are four angels involved in this sixth trumpet judgment, because the number four refers to the whole world: there are four directions, four corners, four winds, etc. These four angels loose judgment upon the *whole world*.

A third part of men are slain by these horsemen. If the earth currently has 7.5 billion people, and one third of them are taken there, you have an idea of how many are involved, how many will die, and how many will be left:

Therefore has the curse devoured the earth, and they that dwell therein are desolate: therefore the inhabitants of the earth are burned, and few men left. (Isaiah 24:6)

The sixth plague will be unprecedented:

And at that time shall Michael stand up, the great prince which stands for the children of your people: and there shall be a time of trouble, such as never was since there was a nation even to that same time: and at that time your people shall be delivered, every one that shall be found written in the book. (Daniel 12:1)

But there will be no repentance. The great moral sin that will be involved here is fornication or sexual sins. This will be the same as the period preceding the flood and Sodom and Gomorrah. It will be a terrible day of devastation—the day of the Lord, or the day of God's wrath.

CHAPTER TEN

In chapters 10 and 11, we see preparations for the physical return of Jesus. Who is this *"mighty angel"* in the first two verses of chapter 10 who stands on the sea and the earth? This is undoubtedly Jesus Christ. He is a mighty angel, which refers to the *Almighty*. He is clothed with a cloud, which refers only to deity:

And it came to pass on the third day in the morning, that there were thunders and lightnings, and a thick cloud upon the mount, and the voice of the trumpet exceeding loud; so that all the people that was in the camp trembled. (Exodus 19:16)

And then shall appear the sign of the Son of man in heaven: and then shall all the tribes of the earth mourn, and they shall see the Son of man coming in the clouds of heaven with power and great glory. (Matthew 24:30)

Behold, He comes with clouds; and every eye shall see Him, and they also which pierced Him: and all kindreds of the earth shall wail because of Him. Even so, Amen. (Revelation 1:7)

REVELATION 10

¹And I saw another mighty angel come down from heaven, clothed with a cloud: and a rainbow was upon his head, and his face was as it were the sun, and his feet as pillars of fire:

²and he had in his hand a little book open: and he set his right foot upon the sea, and his left foot on the earth,

³and cried with a loud voice, as when a lion roars: and when he had cried, seven thunders uttered their voices.

⁴And when the seven thunders had uttered their voices, I was about to write: and I heard a voice from heaven saying to me, Seal up those things which the seven thunders uttered, and write them not.

⁵And the angel which I saw stand upon the sea and upon the earth lifted up his hand to heaven,

⁶and swore by Him that lives for ever and ever, who created heaven, and the things that therein are, and the earth, and the things that therein are, and the sea, and the things which are therein, that there should be time no longer:

⁷but in the days of the voice of the seventh angel, when he shall begin to sound, the mystery of God should be finished, as He has declared to His servants the prophets.

⁸And the voice which I heard from heaven spoke to me again, and said,

Go and take the little book which is open in the hand of the angel which stands upon the sea and upon the earth.

⁹And I went to the angel, and said to him, Give me the little book. And he said to me, Take it, and eat it up; and it shall make your belly bitter, but it shall be in your mouth sweet as honey.

¹⁰And I took the little book out of the angel's hand, and ate it up; and it was in my mouth sweet as honey: and as soon as I had eaten it, my belly was bitter.

¹¹And he said to me, You must prophesy again before many peoples, and nations, and tongues, and kings.

NOTES

_____

_____

_____

_____

_____

_____

_____

_____

_____

_____

_____

He has a rainbow around His head. The rainbow is a sign of God's promise to redeem the earth. The rainbow always shows God's relationship with earth—referring back to His covenant with Noah in Genesis 9:11–17.

Remember the theme of this book: God is showing us that Christ is taking hold and possession of the earth once again. In the beginning, the earth belonged to man. (See Genesis 1:26–28.) This "repossession" by Christ is symbolized by the angel's right foot on the sea and His left foot on the earth. Every place on which the soles of our feet tread is to be ours:

> Every place whereon the soles of your feet shall tread shall be yours: from the wilderness and Lebanon, from the river, the river Euphrates, even to the uttermost sea shall your coast be.
> (Deuteronomy 11:24)

> Every place that the sole of your foot shall tread upon, that have I given to you, as I said to Moses. (Joshua 1:3)

The angel's face is described like the sun. Christ's countenance was described in a similar manner earlier:

> And He had in His right hand seven stars: and out of His mouth went a sharp two edged sword: and His countenance was as the sun shines in His strength. (Revelation 1:16)

At the Transfiguration, Jesus's face shone in a similar manner:

> And was transfigured before them: and His face did shine as the sun, and His raiment was white as the light. (Matthew 17:2)

Christ is also described as the *"Sun"* in the Old Testament:

But to you that fear My name shall the Sun of righteousness arise with healing in His wings; and you shall go forth, and grow up as calves of the stall. (Malachi 4:2)

The angel's feet are described as pillars of fire, similar to the description of Jesus's feet in chapter one:

And His feet like to fine brass, as if they burned in a furnace; and His voice as the sound of many waters. (Revelation 1:15)

He is, of course, the Lion of the tribe of Judah:

And one of the elders says to me, Weep not: behold, the Lion of the tribe of Juda, the Root of David, has prevailed to open the book, and to loose the seven seals thereof. (Revelation 5:5)

And cried with a loud voice, as when a lion roars.... (Revelation 10:3)

The *"time no longer,"* mentioned in verse 6, simply means there shall be no more delay. The seventh trumpet, like the seventh vial, will bring us to the end of the time of trouble.

The book John eats (see verse 10) is the title deed to the earth. The *"little book"* is undoubtedly the book of chapter 5. The book's contents will not only be sweet to John when he eats it, but it will also be bitter, because he has to be a part of getting the earth in order by way of the judgments.

The little book is in the center of the book of Revelation. The earth will be reclaimed. John is to eat the book and *"prophesy again"* (verse 11). Why?

Because man will be given dominion of the earth again; the saints are destined to inherit the earth:

In whom also we have obtained an inheritance, being predestinated according to the purpose of Him who works all things after the counsel of His own will: that we should be to the praise of His glory, who first trusted in Christ. In whom you also trusted, after that you heard the word of truth, the gospel of your salvation: in whom also after that you believed, you were sealed with that holy Spirit of promise, which is the earnest of our inheritance until the redemption of the purchased possession, to the praise of His glory.
(Ephesians 1:11–14)

This is fulfilled at the sounding of the seventh trumpet:

And the seventh angel sounded; and there were great voices in heaven, saying, The kingdoms of this world are become the kingdoms of our Lord, and of His Christ; and He shall reign for ever and ever. (Revelation 11:15)

And the kingdom and dominion, and the greatness of the kingdom under the whole heaven, shall be given to the people of the saints of the Most High, whose kingdom is an everlasting kingdom, and all dominions shall serve and obey Him. (Daniel 7:27)

How many men—Napoleon, Hitler, Mussolini—have dreamed of conquering the world? Many! But God will give the world to the saints; it is our inheritance.

We will soon see the response of the inhabitants of earth and of Satan to the trumpet judgments!

CHAPTER ELEVEN

In chapter 10, we saw the *legal* possession of the earth by man; in chapter 11, we will see the *physical* possession of the earth by Christ. John is given *"a reed like unto a rod"* (Revelation 11:1) and told to *"measure the temple."* Thus, it was at the same time a measuring instrument and an instrument of judgment. Judgment must begin at God's house:

> *For the time is come that judgment must begin at the house of God: and if it first begin at us, what shall the end be of them that obey not the gospel of God?* (1 Peter 4:17)

The temple at this time will be the Tribulation Temple. It will be in Jerusalem.

According to historical records, Julian the Apostate sought to make prophecy of no effect by permitting the Jews to rebuild the temple in AD 363, but history also records that balls of fire came up out of the earth and put a stop to his efforts.

The history of the temple began with David. He desired to build it, but God only let him prepare for it. Solomon built the first temple, and the *shekinah* glory of God appeared in it. When the Jews would

¹And there was given me a reed like to a rod: and the angel stood, saying, Rise, and measure the temple of God, and the altar, and them that worship therein.

²But the court which is outside the temple leave out, and measure it not; for it is given to the Gentiles: and the holy city shall they tread under foot forty and two months.

³And I will give power to my two witnesses, and they shall prophesy a thousand two hundred and three-score days, clothed in sackcloth.

⁴These are the two olive trees, and the two candlesticks standing before the God of the earth.

⁵And if any man will hurt them, fire proceeds out of their mouth, and devours their enemies: and if any man will hurt them, he must in this manner be killed.

⁶These have power to shut heaven, that it rain not in the days of their prophecy: and have power over waters to turn them to blood, and to smite the earth with all plagues, as often as they will.

⁷And when they shall have finished their testimony, the beast that ascends out of the bottomless pit shall make war against them, and shall overcome them, and kill them.

⁸And their dead bodies shall lie in the street of the great city, which spiritually is called Sodom and

Egypt, where also our Lord was crucified.

⁹And they of the people and kindreds and tongues and nations shall see their dead bodies three days and a half, and shall not permit their dead bodies to be put in graves.

¹⁰And they that dwell upon the earth shall rejoice over them, and make merry, and shall send gifts one to another; because these two prophets tormented them that dwelt on the earth.

¹¹And after three days and a half the Spirit of life from God entered into them, and they stood upon their feet; and great fear fell upon them which saw them.

¹²And they heard a great voice from heaven saying to them, Come up here. And they ascended up to heaven in a cloud; and their enemies beheld them.

¹³And the same hour was there a great earthquake, and the tenth part of the city fell, and in the earthquake were slain of men seven thousand: and the remnant were frightened, and gave glory to the God of heaven.

¹⁴The second woe is past; and, behold, the third woe comes quickly.

¹⁵And the seventh angel sounded; and there were great voices in heaven, saying, The kingdoms of this world are become the kingdoms of our Lord, and of His

not repent of their idolatry, however, their temple was razed by Nebuchadnezzar. Seventy years later, when they returned to their land, they built another temple that was inferior to Solomon's temple.

About forty years before Jesus was born, Herod renovated and added to the temple. It was called "Herod's temple":

> *Then said the Jews, Forty and six years was this temple in building, and will You rear it up in three days?* (John 2:20)

Jesus, however, prophesied that Herod's temple would be destroyed. This was fulfilled in AD 70 by Titus, a Roman general. However, an end-time temple was also prophesied by Jesus:

> *When you therefore shall see the abomination of desolation, spoken of by Daniel the prophet, stand in the holy place, (whoso reads, let him understand:).* (Matthew 24:15)

The abomination of desolation was to be set up in the Holy of Holies. Paul prophesied of this in 2 Thessalonians 2:1–13.

When the Jews rebuild the temple, it will again be the reflection of Christ:

> *What? know you not that your body is the temple of the Holy Ghost which is in you, which you have of God, and you are not your own? For you are bought with a price: therefore glorify God in your body, and in your spirit, which are God's.* (1 Corinthians 6:19–20)

The Jews, under the Antichrist, will rebuild their temple and offer sacrifices again. In the midst of the tribulation period, Antichrist will break his agreement with the Jews and set up his idol in the temple:

And he shall confirm the covenant with many for one week: and in the midst of the week he shall cause the sacrifice and the oblation to cease, and for the overspreading of abominations he shall make it desolate, even until the consummation, and that determined shall be poured upon the desolate. (Daniel 9:27)

When you therefore shall see the abomination of desolation, spoken of by Daniel the prophet, stand in the holy place, (whoso reads, let him understand:) then let them which be in Judaea flee into the mountains. (Matthew 24:15–16)

For then shall be great tribulation, such as was not since the beginning of the world to this time, no, nor ever shall be. And except those days should be shortened, there should no flesh be saved: but for the elect's sake those days shall be shortened. Then if any man shall say to you. Lo, here is Christ, or there; believe it not. (Matthew 24:21–23)

Let no man deceive you by any means: for that day shall not come, except there come a falling away first, and that man of sin be revealed, the son of perdition; who opposes and exalts himself above all that is called god, or that is worshiped; so that he as god sits in the temple of God, showing himself that he is god. (2 Thessalonians 2:3–4)

Please note that *"abomination"* almost always refers to idolatry:

For Solomon went after Ashtoreth the goddess of the Zidonians, and after Milcom the abomination of the Ammonites. And Solomon did

Christ; and He shall reign for ever and ever.

16 And the four and twenty elders, which sat before God on their seats, fell upon their faces, and worshiped God,

17 saying, We give You thanks, O Lord God Almighty, which are, and were, and are to come; because You have taken to You Your great power, and have reigned.

18 And the nations were angry, and Your wrath is come, and the time of the dead, that they should be judged, and that You should give reward to Your servants the prophets, and to the saints, and them that fear Your name, small and great; and should destroy them which destroy the earth.

19 And the temple of God was opened in heaven, and there was seen in His temple the ark of His testament: and there were lightnings, and voices, and thunderings, and an earthquake, and great hail.

NOTES

_____

_____

_____

_____

_____

_____

_____

———————————————

———————————————

———————————————

———————————————

———————————————

———————————————

———————————————

———————————————

———————————————

———————————————

———————————————

———————————————

———————————————

———————————————

———————————————

———————————————

———————————————

———————————————

———————————————

———————————————

———————————————

———————————————

evil in the sight of the Lord, *and went not fully after the* Lord, *as did David his father. Then did Solomon build a high place for Chemosh, the abomination of Moab, in the hill that is before Jerusalem, and for Molech, the abomination of the children of Ammon.*   (1 Kings 11:5–7)

And He brought me into the inner court of the Lord's *house, and, behold, at the door of the temple of the* Lord, *between the porch and the altar, were about five and twenty men, with their backs toward the temple of the* Lord, *and their faces toward the east; and they worshiped the sun toward the east. Then He said to me, Have you seen this, O son of man? Is it a light thing to the house of Judah that they commit the abominations which they commit here? for they have filled the land with violence, and have returned to provoke Me to anger: and, lo, they put the branch to their nose.*   (Ezekiel 8:16–17)

And deceives them that dwell on the earth by the means of those miracles which he had power to do in the sight of the beast; saying to them that dwell on the earth, that they should make an image to the beast, which had the wound by a sword, and did live. And he had power to give life to the image of the beast, that the image of the beast should both speak, and cause that as many as would not worship the image of the beast should be killed.   (Revelation 13:14–15)

On earth, once Satan has brought forth his Antichrist, we will see Jacob's trouble:

For thus says the Lord; *We have heard a voice of trembling, of fear, and not of peace. Ask you now, and see whether a man does travail with child? why do I see every man with his hands on his loins, as a woman in travail, and all faces are turned into paleness? Alas! for that day is great, so that none is like it: it is even the time of Jacob's trouble; but he shall be saved out of it.*

(Jeremiah 30:5–7)

And he shall confirm the covenant with many for one week: and in the midst of the week he shall cause the sacrifice and the oblation to cease, and for the overspreading of abominations he shall make it desolate, even until the consummation, and that determined shall be poured upon the desolate. (Daniel 9:27)

And they shall fall by the edge of the sword, and shall be led away captive into all nations: and Jerusalem shall be trodden down of the Gentiles, until the times of the Gentiles be fulfilled.

(Luke 21:24)

The godly Jews flee into the wilderness, to Edom and Moab. Zechariah 14:4 tells of an earthquake at the time of the Second Coming, which will split the mount of Olives in two sections, resulting in a great valley. Because the Mosque of Omar and the Tribulation Temple would be near this earthquake, they may be destroyed.

Before the seventh trumpet is sounded, two unique witnesses begin their testimony in Jerusalem. The two witnesses appear, coming against Antichrist and what he is trying to do. The two witnesses harass the Antichrist. They reenact the life, death, and resurrection of Jesus (See Revelation 11:11–12). This will make a tremendous impact on the world, and especially on the Jews. An earthquake attended Jesus's death and resurrection, and one will also attend the death and resurrection of the two witnesses:

And, behold, the veil of the temple was rent in two from the top to the bottom; and the earth did quake, and the rocks rent. (Matthew 27:51)	*And the same hour was there a great earthquake, and the tenth part of the city fell, and in the earthquake were slain of men seven thousand: and the remnant were frightened, and gave glory to the God of heaven.* (Revelation 11:13)

At Jesus's death, it was still a day of grace and mercy. This day will be a day of judgment: seven thousand will be killed, and people will be terrified.

Who are the two witnesses? We see them on the Mount of Transfiguration:

And as He prayed, the fashion of His countenance was altered, and His raiment was white and glistering. And, behold, there talked with Him two men, which were Moses and Elijah.
(Luke 9:29–30)

We see them after the Resurrection:

But Mary stood outside at the sepulcher weeping: and as she wept, she stooped down, and looked into the sepulcher, and sees two angels in white sitting, the one at the head, and the other at the feet, where the body of Jesus had lain.
(John 20:11–12)

We see them at the Ascension:

And while they looked steadfastly toward heaven as He went up, behold, two men stood by them in white apparel. (Acts 1:10)

Malachi prophesied of one of these witnesses:

Behold, I will send you Elijah the prophet before the coming of the great and dreadful day of the Lord: and he shall turn the heart of the fathers to the children, and the heart of the children to their fathers, lest I come and smite the earth with a curse. (Malachi 4:5–6)

They smite the earth with a curse just like Elijah closed the heavens and Moses brought the plagues. (See 1 Kings 17:1; Exodus 7–12.)

These two witnesses prophesy during the last three-and-one-half years of the tribulation. Their ascension before the eyes of their enemies brings to an end the second woe, which began with the sixth trumpet. (See Revelation 9:13.)

7

Now we are ready for the seventh trumpet judgment. As before every great event, there is a worship service in heaven led by the elders:

And the four and twenty elders, which sat before God on their seats, fell upon their faces, and worshiped God. (Revelation 11:16)

In verse 18, we are told that *"the nations were angry."* This anticipates Armageddon.

The ark of the covenant is seen in verse 19. Remember, the ark was always used to lead God's people to victory.

The final earthquake, mentioned in Revelation 11:19, will be the worst since creation. Whatever is left

_____

_____

_____

_____

_____

_____

_____

_____

_____

_____

_____

_____

_____

_____

_____

_____

_____

_____

_____

_____

_____

_____

_____

_____

after the first six trumpet judgments will be destroyed by hail—heavy stones weighing perhaps sixty pounds each. This will be in God's plan of reconstruction by Christ and His saints. Israel is to be refined by fire:

> And I will bring the third part through the fire, and will refine them as silver is refined, and will try them as gold is tried: they shall call on My name, and I will hear them: I will say, It is My people: and they shall say, The LORD is my God.
>
> (Zechariah 13:9)

CHAPTER TWELVE

We are going to look at the twelfth chapter in parallel with the fourth chapter. Jesus said that every word would be established *"in the mouth of two or three witnesses"* (Matthew 18:16). The book of Revelation from chapter 12 to chapter 16 gives a *second* witness to chapters 4–11. Chapters 17 and 18 give a *third* witness.

Now we will see, as John saw, the Antichrist and the events of Revelation 4–11, from an *earthly* viewpoint:

I tell you, in that night there shall be two men in one bed; the one shall be taken, and the other shall be left. Two women shall be grinding together; the one shall be taken, and the other left. Two men shall be in the field; the one shall be taken, and the other left. (Luke 17:34–36)

And at that time shall Michael stand up, the great prince which stands for the children of your people: and there shall be a time of trouble, such as never was since there was a nation even to that same time: and at that time your people shall be delivered, every one that shall be found written

REVELATION 12

[1]And there appeared a great wonder in heaven; a woman clothed with the sun, and the moon under her feet, and upon her head a crown of twelve stars:

[2]and she being with child cried, travailing in birth, and pained to be delivered.

[3]And there appeared another wonder in heaven; and behold a great red dragon, having seven heads and ten horns, and seven crowns upon his heads.

[4]And his tail drew the third part of the stars of heaven, and did cast them to the earth: and the dragon stood before the woman which was ready to be delivered, for to devour her child as soon as it was born.

[5]And she brought forth a man child, who was to rule all nations with a rod of iron: and her child was caught up to God, and to His throne.

NOTES

_____

_____

_____

_____

_____

_____

_____

_____

_____

_____

_____

_____

_____

_____

_____

_____

_____

_____

_____

_____

_____

_____

_____

_____

_____

_____

_____

_____

_____

_____

_____

_____

_____

in the book. And many of them that sleep in the dust of the earth shall awake, some to everlasting life, and some to shame and everlasting contempt. And they that be wise shall shine as the brightness of the firmament; and they that turn many to righteousness as the stars for ever and ever. (Daniel 12:1–3)

John saw a great wonder—a woman in the sky clothed with the sun, with the moon under her feet, and a crown of twelve stars upon her head. This woman symbolizes the church, which is comprised of all born-again believers. This woman is a representation of the church mentioned earlier in chapters 2 and 3. Let's look at several reasons why we know this woman symbolizes the church:

1. She is *"clothed with the sun"* (Revelation 12:1). This is a clear picture of the church being clothed with Christ. The prophet Malachi described Jesus as *"the Sun"*:

But to you that fear My name shall the Sun of righteousness arise with healing in His wings; and you shall go forth, and grow up as calves of the stall. (Malachi 4:2)

Jesus called Himself *"the light of the world"*:

Then spoke Jesus again to them, saying, I am the light of the world: he that follows Me shall not walk in darkness, but shall have the light of life. (John 8:12)

Jesus also said that the church is the light of the world:

You are the light of the world. A city that is set on a hill cannot be hidden. (Matthew 5:14)

God's light is given to us through Jesus, His Word, and the power of the Holy Spirit:

Your word is a lamp to my feet, and a light to my path. (Psalm 119:105)

Peter confirmed that the church is a people clothed with light:

But you are a chosen generation, a royal priesthood, a holy nation, a peculiar people; that you should show forth the praises of Him who has called you out of darkness into His marvellous light. (1 Peter 2:9)

2. She has *"the moon under her feet"* (Revelation 12:1). The church is victorious; darkness and error are under her feet :

Behold, I give to you power to tread on serpents and scorpions, and over all the power of the enemy: and nothing shall by any means hurt you. (Luke 10:19)

And has put all things under His feet, and gave Him to be the head over all things to the church, Which is His body, the fullness of Him that fills all in all. (Ephesians 1:22–23)

3. The woman wears *"a crown of twelve stars"* (Revelation 12:1). These stars represent the church's leadership, just as the twelve apostles were the leadership of the early church:

And Jesus said to them, Verily I say to you, That you which have followed Me, in the regeneration when the Son of Man shall sit in the throne of His glory, you also shall sit upon twelve thrones, judging the twelve tribes of Israel.
(Matthew 19:28)

In Revelation 12:2, we read that the woman is *"with child"* and *"travailing in birth."* Paul used the symbol of a woman in travail in 1 Thessalonians:

For when they shall say, Peace and safety; then sudden destruction comes upon them, as travail upon a woman with child; and they shall not escape. (1 Thessalonians 5:3)

Isaiah and Ezekiel mention this travail:

A voice of noise from the city, a voice from the temple, a voice of the Lord that renders recompence to His enemies. Before she travailed, she brought forth; before her pain came, she was delivered of a man child. Who has heard such a thing? who has seen such things? Shall the earth be made to bring forth in one day? or shall a nation be born at once? for as soon as Zion travailed, she brought forth her children. (Isaiah 66:6–8)

Then He said to me, Son of man, these bones are the whole house of Israel: behold, they say, Our bones are dried, and our hope is lost: we are cut off for our parts. Therefore prophesy and say to them, Thus says the Lord God; Behold, O My people, I will open your graves, and cause you to come up out of your graves, and bring you into the land of Israel. And you shall know that I am the Lord, when I have opened your graves, O My people, and brought you up out of your graves, And shall put My Spirit in you, and you shall live, and I shall place you in your own land: then shall you know that I the Lord have spoken it, and performed it, says the Lord. (Ezekiel 37:11–14)

The woman's seed will bruise the head of the serpent:

And I will put enmity between you and the woman, and between your seed and her seed; it shall bruise your head, and you shall bruise his heel. (Genesis 3:15)

Satan has always known this and therefore tried to devour the seed of the woman. In the days of Moses, the Israelite male babies were ordered to be killed. Look at the days of King Herod, when the children of Bethlehem were ordered slain. Satan tried to kill the promised seed.

God saw ahead to what Satan would try to do to His creation and provided a secret plan for their redemption, which was hidden even from the angels:

Searching what, or what manner of time the Spirit of Christ which was in them did signify, when it testified beforehand the sufferings of Christ, and the glory that should follow. To whom it was revealed, that not to themselves, but to us they did minister the things, which are now reported to you by them that have preached the gospel to you with the Holy Ghost sent down from heaven; which things the angels desire to look into. (1 Peter 1:11–12)

In Revelation 12:5, we see a separation between the woman and her child. Not only is the woman a symbol of the church, but the child is also symbolic of the church. The man child (Christ and His church) is to rule over the nations:

I will declare the decree: the LORD has said to me, You are My Son; this day have I begotten You. Ask of Me, and I shall give You the heathen for

Your inheritance, and the uttermost parts of the earth for your possession. You shall break them with a rod of iron; You shall dash them in pieces like a potter's vessel. (Psalm 2:7–9)

And he that overcomes, and keeps My works to the end, to him will I give power over the nations: and he shall rule them with a rod of iron; as the vessels of a potter shall they be broken to shivers: even as I received of My Father. (Revelation 2:26–27)

The child is *"caught up"* to God's throne to escape Satan. This is a picture of the rapture:

For the Lord Himself shall descend from heaven with a shout, with the voice of the archangel, and with the trump of God: and the dead in Christ shall rise first: then we which are alive and remain shall be caught up together with them in the clouds, to meet the Lord in the air: and so shall we ever be with the Lord. (1 Thessalonians 4:16–17)

Remember, these three signals at the resurrection of the saved dead at the time of the rapture: the shout, the voice of the archangel, and the trump of God. Isaiah 66:6–8 (quoted previously) also speaks of these three signals: the noise from the city, a voice out of the temple, and the Lord's voice. The woman brings forth a *man child*. After that, she brings forth her children. A *"man child"* is the picture of the rapture of the church, and the "children" are the ones saved after the rapture—during the tribulation.

In the days of Elijah, the sons of the prophets had a premonition that he would be taken:

And the sons of the prophets that were at Jericho came to Elisha, and said to him, Know you that the LORD will take away your master from your head today? And he answered, Yea, I know it; hold you your peace. (2 Kings 2:5)

Yet, when the event occurred, they were not ready to believe that it had taken place. They were convinced that Elijah had not gone all the way to heaven. Obadiah for example, thought Elijah had been transported to another place:

And it shall come to pass, as soon as I am gone from you, that the Spirit of the LORD shall carry you where I know not; and so when I come and tell Ahab, and he cannot find you he shall slay me: but I your servant fear the LORD from my youth. (1 Kings 18:12)

Elisha protested when fifty men began to search, but they did it anyway:

And they said to him, Behold now, there be with your servants fifty strong men; let them go, we pray you, and seek your master: lest perhaps the Spirit of the LORD has taken him up, and cast him upon some mountain, or into some valley. And he said, You shall not send. And when they urged him till he was ashamed, he said, Send. They sent therefore fifty men; and they sought three days, but found him not.
(2 Kings 2:16–17)

Perhaps these three days are a picture of the three years of the great tribulation.

Later, when news came to Bethel that Elisha was coming, some young people came out and said, "Go up, you bald head; go up" (2 Kings 2:23). They were mocking the rapture of Elijah, but God certainly brought vengeance upon them. Two ferocious bears came out and destroyed forty-two of them—just as two beasts in Revelation will arise in the tribulation to terrorize for forty-two months. In Revelation 13, the beast has the feet of a bear. Today, Russia is sometimes symbolized by a bear.

At any rate, when the resurrection of the saved dead and the rapture of the living saints occur, it will be a tremendous undertaking, and the powers of the heavens will be involved. Miracles will be used to protect this "child."

When the church is caught up, a lot of things will happen. Remember, there will be millions arriving in heaven at the same time. It will be different than ever before. This ruling class will take over with Jesus Christ and will share His throne.

When the church arrives in heaven, it spells the downfall of Satan. Since Satan has always occupied the area between the earth and heaven, he is in a good place to devour the child as soon as it is born. But God will shake him out:

> For thus says the LORD of hosts; Yet once, it is a little while, and I will shake the heavens, and the earth, and the sea, and the dry land; and I will shake all nations, and the desire of all nations shall come: and I will fill this house with glory, says the LORD of hosts. (Haggai 2:6–7)

> Whose voice then shook the earth: but now He has promised, saying, Yet once more I shake not the earth only, but also heaven. And this word, Yet once more, signifies the removing of those things that are shaken, as of things that are

made, that those things which cannot be shaken
may remain. (Hebrews 12:26–27)

Who is *Michael* mentioned in Revelation 12:7?
He is the leader of God's angelic forces:

And at that time shall Michael stand up, the
great prince which stands for the children of your
people: and there shall be a time of trouble, such
as never was since there was a nation even to
that same time: and at that time your people
shall be delivered, every one that shall be found
written in the book.
(Daniel 12:1; see also Daniel 10:13–21)

Michael will stand up for the raptured saints. He
will war against Satan, just as he warred against Satan
for Moses's body. The catching away of the man child
has a definite connection with Satan's defeat and over-
throw in the heavenlies.

There was a "court trial" when Michael contended
for the body of Moses (See Jude 1:9), but we will have
Jesus as our attorney:

My little children, these things write I to you,
that you sin not. And if any man sin, we have an
advocate with the Father, Jesus Christ the righ-
teous. (1 John 2:1)

The resulting expulsion of Satan from heaven to
the earth in Revelation 12:7–9 will bring great persecution by the Antichrist on the people who are saved
during the tribulation period; there will be many
martyrs:

And except those days should be shortened, there
should no flesh be saved: but for the elect's sake
those days shall be shortened. (Matthew 24:22)

And white robes were given to every one of them; and it was said to them, that they should rest yet for a little season, until their fellow-servants also and their brethren, that should be killed as they were, should be fulfilled. (Revelation 6:11)

And it was given to him [the dragon] *to make war with the saints, and to overcome them: and power was given him over all kindreds, and tongues, and nations.* (Revelation 13:7)

The *"stars"* in Revelation 12:4, which follow Satan, are the fallen angels. A third part of the *"stars"* are fallen angels pulled by Satan, who is called Lucifer *"son of the morning,"* or "morning star" in Isaiah 14:12. These angels comprise Satan's government today.

Satan and the powers of darkness are presently dwelling in the *heavenlies.* (Not in God's *heaven,* but the space above the earth.) The time will soon come when he will be displaced from the heavenlies to the earth, to fiercely persecute the saints during the tribulation.

Satan was cast out of God's heaven as his *dwelling* place long ago:

How are you fallen from heaven, O Lucifer, son of the morning! how are you cut down to the ground, which did weaken the nations! For you have said in your heart, I will ascend into heaven, I will exalt my throne above the stars of God: I will sit also upon the mount of the congregation, in the sides of the north: I will ascend above the heights of the clouds; I will be like the Most High. Yet you shall be brought down to hell, to the sides of the pit. (Isaiah 14:12–15)

Satan, however, still has *access* to heaven until a future time:

> *And I heard a loud voice saying in heaven, Now is come salvation, and strength, and the kingdom of our God, and the power of His Christ: for the accuser of our brethren is cast down, which accused them before our God day and night.*
> (Revelation 12:10; see also Job 1:6–12)

After the rapture, there will be great persecution—falling stars, pestilences, earthquakes, plagues—and they will come to hinder the dragon and to help the woman. Chapter 13 gives details of Satan's persecution on those people who are saved during the tribulation.

The *"flood"* mentioned in Revelation 12:15 refers to armies:

> *Who is this that comes up as a flood, whose waters are moved as the rivers? Egypt rises up like a flood, and his waters are moved like the rivers; and he said, I will go up, and will cover the earth; I will destroy the city and the inhabitants thereof.* (Jeremiah 46:7–8)

> *Thus says the LORD; Behold, waters rise up out of the north, and shall be an overflowing flood, and shall overflow the land, and all that is therein; the city, and them that dwell therein: then the men shall cry, and all the inhabitants of the land shall howl.* (Jeremiah 47:2)

An understanding of Jesus's words in Matthew 24 will help us put this whole time period in focus:

> *And Jesus went out, and departed from the temple: and His disciples came to Him for to show Him the buildings of the temple. And*

Jesus said to them, See you not all these things? verily I say to you, There shall not be left here one stone upon another, that shall not be thrown down. And as He sat upon the mount of Olives, the disciples came to Him privately, saying, Tell us, when shall these things be? and what shall be the sign of Your coming, and of the end of the world? (Matthew 24:1–3)

There are three questions in this passage of Scripture:

1. When shall these things be?

2. What shall be the sign of Your coming?

3. What shall be the sign of the end of the world?

The last two questions, of course, are at the end of the age. But the first question has to do with Jerusalem—the destruction of the temple by Titus in AD 70. Jesus tells about this. He gives the answer in Luke:

And when you shall see Jerusalem compassed with armies, then know that the desolation thereof is near. Then let them which are in Judaea flee to the mountains; and let them which are in the midst of it depart out; and let not them that are in the countries enter thereto. For these be the days of vengeance, that all things which are written may be fulfilled. But woe to them that are with child, and to them that give suck, in those days! for there shall be great distress in the land, and wrath upon this people. And they shall fall by the edge of the sword, and shall be led away captive into all nations: and Jerusalem shall be trodden down of the Gentiles, until the times of the Gentiles be fulfilled.

(Luke 21:20–24)

Jesus also speaks in Matthew 24 of the beginning of the great tribulation with the abomination of desolation:

When you therefore shall see the abomination of desolation, spoken of by Daniel the prophet, stand in the holy place, (whoso reads, let him understand:). (Matthew 24:15)

This is the time for tribulation saints to flee into the wilderness, but God will shorten the time for the elect's sake. Jesus also warned against the beast and false prophet.

For there shall arise false Christs, and false prophets, and shall show great signs and wonders; insomuch that, if it were possible, they shall deceive the very elect. Behold, I have told you before. Wherefore if they shall say to you, Behold, He is in the desert; go not forth: behold, He is in the secret chambers; believe it not. (Matthew 24:24–26)

With the darkening of the sun, and with the moon becoming as blood, we have the end of the tribulation, and the beginning of the day of God's wrath:

And I beheld when He had opened the sixth seal, and, lo, there was a great earthquake; and the sun became black as sackcloth of hair, and the moon became as blood; And the stars of heaven fell to the earth, even as a fig tree casts her untimely figs, when she is shaken of a mighty wind. And the heaven departed as a scroll when it is rolled together; and every mountain and island were moved out of their places. And the kings of the earth, and the great men, and the rich men, and the chief captains, and the mighty men, and every bondman, and every free man,

REVELATION 12

⁶And the woman fled into the wilderness, where she has a place prepared of God, that they should feed her there a thousand two hundred and threescore days.

⁷And there was war in heaven: Michael and his angels fought against the dragon; and the dragon fought and his angels,

⁸and prevailed not; neither was their place found any more in heaven.

⁹And the great dragon was cast out, that old serpent, called the Devil, and Satan, which deceives the whole world: he was cast out into the earth, and his angels were cast out with him.

¹⁰And I heard a loud voice saying in heaven, Now is come salvation, and strength, and the kingdom of our God, and the power of His Christ: for the accuser of our brethren is cast down, which accused them before our God day and night.

¹¹And they overcame him by the blood of the Lamb, and by the word of their testimony; and they loved not their lives to the death.

¹²Therefore rejoice, you heavens, and you that dwell in them. Woe to the inhabiters of the earth and of the sea! for the devil is come down to you, having great wrath, because he knows that he has but a short time.

¹³And when the dragon saw that he was cast to the earth, he persecuted

the woman which brought forth the man child.

¹⁴And to the woman were given two wings of a great eagle, that she might fly into the wilderness, into her place, where she is nourished for a time, and times, and half a time, from the face of the serpent.

¹⁵And the serpent cast out of his mouth water as a flood after the woman, that he might cause her to be carried away of the flood.

¹⁶And the earth helped the woman, and the earth opened her mouth, and swallowed up the flood which the dragon cast out of his mouth.

¹⁷And the dragon was angry with the woman, and went to make war with the remnant of her seed, which keep the commandments of God, and have the testimony of Jesus Christ.

NOTES

_____

_____

_____

_____

_____

_____

_____

_____

_____

hid themselves in the dens and in the rocks of the mountains; and said to the mountains and rocks, Fall on us, and hide us from the face of Him that sits on the throne, and from the wrath of the Lamb: for the great day of His wrath is come; and who shall be able to stand?
(Revelation 6:12–17)

The sun shall be turned into darkness, and the moon into blood, before that great and notable day of the Lord come. (Acts 2:20)

After these celestial disturbances, we see the coming of Christ for His elect; it is the harvest rapture and resurrection, which follows the opening of the sixth seal recorded in Revelation 7:9–14.

The earth will be very corrupt:

But as the days of Noah were, so shall also the coming of the son of man be. For as in the days that were before the flood they were eating and drinking, marrying and giving in marriage, until the day that Noah entered into the ark, and knew not until the flood came, and took them all away; so shall also the coming of the Son of man be. (Matthew 24:37–39)

The fleeing place of the godly Jews is mentioned by Daniel:

He shall enter also into the glorious land, and many countries shall be overthrown: but these shall escape out of his hand, even Edom, and Moab, and the chief of the children of Ammon.
(Daniel 11:41)

The Holy Land and Egypt will be overrun by marching armies. In the day of Rome, there was an actual wilderness. It was called *Pella*. It was deep in

Edom, far from civilization, a wilderness that had proved a welcome refuge.

God will deal with His people in the wilderness:

Ask you now, and see whether a man does travail with child? why do I see every man with his hands on his loins, as a woman in travail, and all faces are turned into paleness? Alas! for that day is great, so that none is like it: it is even the time of Jacob's trouble; but he shall be saved out of it.
(Jeremiah 30:6–7)

Thus says the LORD, The people which were left of the sword found grace in the wilderness; even Israel, when I went to cause him to rest. The LORD has appeared of old to me, saying, Yea, I have loved you with an everlasting love: therefore with lovingkindness have I drawn you.
(Jeremiah 31:2–3)

And I will bring you out from the people, and will gather you out of the countries wherein you are scattered, with a mighty hand, and with a stretched out arm, and with fury poured out. And I will bring you into the wilderness of the people, and there will I plead with you face to face. Like as I pleaded with your fathers in the wilderness of the land of Egypt, so will I plead with you, says the Lord GOD. And I will cause you to pass under the rod, and I will bring you into the bond of the covenant.
(Ezekiel 20:34–37)

Therefore, behold, I will allure her, and bring her into the wilderness, and speak comfortably to her. (Hosea 2:14)

God will make a covenant with His people.

CHAPTER THIRTEEN

The beast of Revelation 13:1 is the Antichrist. Let's look at him and his so-called kingdom:

Little children, it is the last time: and as you have heard that antichrist shall come, even now are there many antichrists; whereby we know that it is the last time. (1 John 2:18)

For then shall be great tribulation, such as was not since the beginning of the world to this time, no, nor ever shall be…. For there shall arise false Christs, and false prophets, and shall show great signs and wonders; insomuch that, if it were possible, they shall deceive the very elect. Behold, I have told you before. (Matthew 24:21, 24–25)

Let no man deceive you by any means: for that day shall not come, except there come a falling away first, and that man of sin be revealed, the son of perdition; who opposes and exalts himself above all that is called god, or that is worshiped; so that he as god sits in the temple of God, showing himself that he is god…. And now you know what withholds that he might be revealed in his time. (2 Thessalonians 2:3–4, 6)

REVELATION 13

¹And I stood upon the sand of the sea, and saw a beast rise up out of the sea, having seven heads and ten horns, and upon his horns ten crowns, and upon his heads the name of blasphemy.

²And the beast which I saw was like to a leopard, and his feet were as the feet of a bear, and his mouth as the mouth of a lion: and the dragon gave him his power, and his seat, and great authority.

NOTES

_____

_____

_____

_____

_____

_____

_____

_____

_____

_____

_____

_____

_____

_____

_____

And he opened his mouth in blasphemy against God, to blaspheme His name, and His tabernacle, and them that dwell in heaven.

(Revelation 13:6)

The Antichrist will blaspheme those that have been raptured into heaven, and he will make war with those on earth.

Daniel chapters 2 and 7 contain a great deal about the Antichrist and a revival of the Roman Empire. Notice that the beast in Revelation 13:1 has all the attributes of the beasts/kingdoms that are described in Daniel 7:4–6: Babylon is like unto a lion; Medo-Persia is like unto a bear; and Greece is like unto a leopard.

Now compare this with Revelation 13:2:

And the beast which I saw was like to a leopard, and his feet were as the feet of a bear, and his mouth as the mouth of a lion: and the dragon gave him his power, and his seat, and great authority.

The leopard, the bear, and the lion—the beast of Revelation 13 combines the ferocity of all three.

To understand the beast and his kingdom, we need to follow the history of the Roman Empire—the two legs of Nebuchadnezzar's image. We will do so with the help of the *Encyclopedia Brittanica* (14th edition):

1. 27 BC — Rome proclaimed an empire with Augustus Caesar its emperor

2. Fourth Century AD — a division occurs between East and West

3. AD 476 — Western empire falls

4. AD 1453 — Eastern empire falls

5. Roman Papacy assumes leadership of the empire from Caesars

6. Odoacer ends the separate rule of the Western Empire, transferring the capital to Constantinople, the "Second Rome," in the East

7. AD 800 — the Pope crowns Charlemagne emperor of the Holy Roman Empire of the West, with its capital at Aix-la-chapelle, Prussia

8. AD 888 — Charlemagne's empire falls, followed by the birth of modern Europe

9. AD 962 — Pope John XII invites Otto I of Germany to assume the imperial crown, thus renewing once again the Roman Empire.

10. AD 1806 — French Revolution and Napoleonic wars end the German Roman Empire—Papacy stripped of its power when Napoleon invades Italy and imprisons the Pope.

11. When the Eastern Empire (Constantinople) falls, the Orthodox Church, under Ivan the Great, moves its center to Moscow. Ivan the Terrible (grandson of Ivan the Great) assumes the title of *Tsar*, thus becoming the successor of the Old Eastern Roman emperor and head of the Orthodox chunch.

12. AD 1917 — The Bolshevik Revolution overthrows the reign of the tsars, ending the institution of the Russian Ortodox Patriarchate of the Greek Church and this phase of the Roman Empire.

Throughout all of this, it is important to see that the Roman empire rose and fell, but each new phase was still a *revival* of the old Roman Empire—it was not a *new empire*. As we shall see, there are more revivals of the Roman Empire according to history, and there will be a future revival of the empire in the days of Antichrist.

13. AD 1935 — Mussolini formally proclaims the restoration of the Roman Empire, and, seeking the favor of the Catholic Church, declares a square mile of territory around the Vatican independent of Italy. After joining forces with Hitler, Mussolini's power begins to decline.

14. AD 1938 — Hitler comes into possession of the crown jewels of the Holy Roman Empire. Seven years later. Hitler's power comes to an end, and with it, another "death" of the Roman Empire.

15. AD 20?? — The Bible indicates that there will be revival of the Greek-Roman Empire before the close of the age, headed by the beast of Revelation 13:1.

Who is the Antichrist or beast of Revelation 13:1? He's an imitator of Christ—the "great pretender."

Jesus prophesied that the Jews would receive the Antichrist:

I am come in My Father's name, and you receive Me not: if another shall come in his own name, him you will receive. (John 5:43)

And with all deceivableness of unrighteousness in them that perish; because they received not the love of the truth, that they might be saved. And for this cause God shall send them strong delusion, that they should believe a lie.
(2 Thessalonians 2:10–11)

The devil tried to offer the world to Christ one time, but Christ turned it down:

And the devil said to Him, All this power will I give You, and the glory of them: for that is delivered to me; and to whomsoever I will I give it. If You therefore will worship me, all shall be Yours. (Luke 4:6–7)

The devil will make the same offer to the Antichrist, and he will eagerly accept it. Now, at last, the devil will receive the worship he so eagerly desires:

And they worshiped the dragon which gave power to the beast: and they worshiped the beast, saying, Who is like to the beast? Who is able to make war with him? (Revelation 13:4)

The Antichrist will use flattery to receive his power:

And in his estate shall stand up a vile person, to whom they shall not give the honor of the kingdom: but he shall come in peaceably, and obtain the kingdom by flatteries. (Daniel 11:21)

He will become strong with a small amount of people:

And after the league made with him he shall work deceitfully: for he shall come up, and shall become strong with a small people. (Daniel 11:23)

The nations will be looking for a leader who will promise peace. There will be a great deal of mystery surrounding this person. However, the world will soon despair over their fateful decision to follow him.

REVELATION 13

³And I saw one of his heads as it were wounded to death; and his deadly wound was healed: and all the world wondered after the beast.

⁴And they worshiped the dragon which gave power to the beast: and they worshiped the beast, saying, Who is like to the beast? Who is able to make war with him?

⁵And there was given to him a mouth speaking great things and blasphemies; and power was given to him to continue forty and two months.

⁶And he opened his mouth in blasphemy against God, to blaspheme His name, and His tabernacle, and them that dwell in heaven.

⁷And it was given to him to make war with the saints, and to overcome them: and power was given him over all kindreds, and tongues, and nations.

⁸And all that dwell upon the earth shall worship him, whose names are not written in the book of life of the Lamb slain from the foundation of the world.

⁹If any man have an ear, let him hear.

¹⁰He that leads into captivity shall go into captivity: he that kills with the sword must be killed with the sword. Here is the patience and the faith of the saints.

¹¹And I beheld another beast coming up out of the earth; and he

What is the significance in Revelation 13:3 of the Antichrist's head being wounded? He "died" from the wound and will appear to rise from the dead—like Jesus. He's the great pretender.

Daniel predicted the Antichrist's death long ago:

> *Then shall stand up in his estate a raiser of taxes in the glory of the kingdom: but within few days he shall be destroyed, neither in anger, nor in battle.* (Daniel 11:20)

What is the end of Satan and the Antichrist? Lake of fire.

Revelation 13:4 reveals humanism at its height— the worship of a man.

What are the activities of the beast in Revelation 13:5–7? He curses, persecutes, and rules the world.

What is the sign of God's coming protection in Revelation 13:6? They are written in the Book of Life.

> *But Christ being come a high priest of good things to come, by a greater and more perfect tabernacle, not made with hands, that is to say, not of this building.* (Hebrews 9:11)

> *And it shall come to pass, when you be multiplied and increased in the land, in those days, says the Lord, they shall say no more, The ark of the covenant of the Lord: neither shall it come to mind: neither shall they remember it; neither shall they visit it; neither shall that be done any more.* (Jeremiah 3:16)

The ark always stands for triumph over the enemies of God; it has a place of importance at the Second Coming of Christ, as we saw at the sounding of the seventh trumpet in Revelation 11:19. In Revelation 15, we read of the angels with the seven vial judgments coming out of the *tabernacle* to deliver God's wrath:

And after that I looked, and, behold, the temple of the tabernacle of the testimony in heaven was opened: and the seven angels came out of the temple, having the seven plagues, clothed in pure and white linen, and having their breasts girded with golden girdles. (Revelation 15:5–6)

What are the activities of the saints in Revelation 13:7–10?

Patience

Faith

The term "Antichrist" appears four times in the Bible. All four occurrences are in 1 and 2 John. The Antichrist will have the mark and a number: 666.

What is the significance of "666"?

The number of evil (man) is 6. Therefore, 666 is a trinity of evil—Satan, the Antichrist, and the false prophet.

had two horns like a lamb, and he spoke as a dragon.

[12]And he exercises all the power of the first beast before him, and causes the earth and them which dwell therein to worship the first beast, whose deadly wound was healed.

[13]And he does great wonders, so that he makes fire come down from heaven on the earth in the sight of men,

[14]and deceives them that dwell on the earth by the means of those miracles which he had power to do in the sight of the beast; saying to them that dwell on the earth, that they should make an image to the beast, which had the wound by a sword, and did live.

[15]And he had power to give life to the image of the beast, that the image of the beast should both speak, and cause that as many as would not worship the image of the beast should be killed.

[16]And he causes all, both small and great, rich and poor, free and bond, to receive a mark in their right hand, or in their foreheads:

[17]and that no man might buy or sell, save he that had the mark, or the name of the beast, or the number of his name.

[18]Here is wisdom. Let him that has understanding count the number of the beast: for it is the number of a man; and his number is Six hundred threescore and six.

CHAPTER FOURTEEN

Revelation 14 deals with the gospel and the tribulation.

In Revelation 14:1–5, we are looking at the earth during an approximate time of three-and-a half years of the tribulation. The 144,000 were sealed with God's name on their foreheads. At this time, remember, the Antichrist is not against Jews; he's confirming his covenant with them. The 144,000 are the firstfruits of the redeemed of Israel. They will become a problem to the Antichrist because they are untouchable. The redeemed sing a song on earth accompanied by heaven. (See verses 2–3.)

There are seven unique things about these 144,000:

1. They are virgins (physically).

2. God's name is written on their foreheads.

3. They sing a special song.

4. They follow the Lamb.

5. They are firstfruits.

6. No guile is in their mouths.

7. They are before God's throne.

REVELATION 14

¹And I looked, and, lo, a Lamb stood on the mount Zion, and with Him a hundred forty and four thousand, having His Father's name written in their foreheads.

²And I heard a voice from heaven, as the voice of many waters, and as the voice of a great thunder: and I heard the voice of harpers harping with their harps:

³and they sung as it were a new song before the throne, and before the four beasts, and the elders: and no man could learn that song but the hundred and forty and four thousand, which were redeemed from the earth.

⁴These are they which were not defiled with women; for they are virgins. These are they which follow the Lamb wherever He goes. These were redeemed from among men, being the first-fruits to God and to the Lamb.

⁵And in their mouth was found no guile: for they are without fault before the throne of God.

⁶And I saw another angel fly in the midst of heaven, having the everlasting gospel to preach to them that dwell on the earth, and to every nation, and kindred, and tongue, and people,

⁷saying with a loud voice, Fear God, and give glory to Him; for the hour of His judgment is come: and worship Him that made heaven, and

earth, and the sea, and the fountains of waters.

[8]And there followed another angel, saying, Babylon is fallen, is fallen, that great city, because she made all nations drink of the wine of the wrath of her fornication.

[9]And the third angel followed them, saying with a loud voice, If any man worship the beast and his image, and receive his mark in his forehead, or in his hand,

[10]the same shall drink of the wine of the wrath of God, which is poured out without mixture into the cup of His indignation; and he shall be tormented with fire and brimstone in the presence of the holy angels, and in the presence of the Lamb:

[11]and the smoke of their torment ascends up for ever and ever: and they have no rest day nor night, who worship the beast and his image, and whosoever receives the mark of his name.

[12]Here is the patience of the saints: here are they that keep the commandments of God, and the faith of Jesus.

[13]And I heard a voice from heaven saying to me, Write, Blessed are the dead which die in the Lord from hereafter: Yea, says the Spirit, that they may rest from their labors; and their works do follow them.

The gospel will be preached during the tribulation. Immediately after the rapture, the first seal is broken. The Rider of the white horse (Christ) goes forth to bring the messages to the earth. He will call upon men of the earth to repent and turn to God. The *"everlasting gospel"* that is preached by the messenger of Revelation 14:6–7 is the same gospel that you and I know. The inhabitants of earth are given ample warning of God's coming judgment; the gospel will be preached in a variety of ways.

God has always warned the world before a great judgment. Noah preached one hundred twenty years before the flood, and demonstrated his faith by building the ark in front of their very eyes. Lot could have been used to preach the gospel to Sodom and Gomorrah if he hadn't become so conformed to the world.

The second messenger (Revelation 14:8) will announce the fall of Babylon. Compare his message with Isaiah's message:

And there followed another angel, saying, Babylon is fallen, is fallen, that great city, because she made all nations drink of the wine of the wrath of her fornication. (Revelation 14:8)	*And, behold, here comes a chariot of men, with a couple of horsemen. And he answered and said, Babylon is fallen, is fallen; and all the graven images of her gods he has broken to the ground.* (Isaiah 21:9)

In the book of Revelation, this is *religious* Babylon. Babylon was always involved with idolatry:

Remove out of the midst of Babylon, and go forth out of the land of the Chaldeans, and be as the he goats before the flocks. (Jeremiah 50:8)

Babylon has been a golden cup in the LORD's hand, that made all the earth drunken: the nations have drunken of her wine; therefore the nations are mad. (Jeremiah 51:7)

Babylon has been a harlot system since the first apostasy after the flood. Nimrod was the founder of Babel:

He was a mighty hunter before the LORD: wherefore it is said, Even as Nimrod the mighty hunter before the LORD. And the beginning of his kingdom was Babel, and Erech, and Accad, and Calneh, in the land of Shinar.
(Genesis 10:9–10)

The great sin of Babylon was idolatry:

A sword is upon the Chaldeans, says the LORD, and upon the inhabitants of Babylon, and upon her princes, and upon her wise men…. A drought is upon her waters; and they shall be dried up: for it is the land of graven images, and they are mad upon their idols.
(Jeremiah 50:35, 38)

The second messenger warns God's people to get out quickly!

The third messenger (see Revelation 14:9–11) warns everyone about the beast and against taking his mark. The consequences of taking his mark are most severe.

In Revelation 14:12–13, we read of the faith and perseverance of the saints. There will be special honor

REVELATION 14

¹⁴And I looked, and behold a white cloud, and upon the cloud one sat like to the Son of man, having on His head a golden crown, and in His hand a sharp sickle.

¹⁵And another angel came out of the temple, crying with a loud voice to Him that sat on the cloud, Thrust in Your sickle, and reap: for the time is come for You to reap; for the harvest of the earth is ripe.

¹⁶And He that sat on the cloud thrust in His sickle on the earth; and the earth was reaped.

¹⁷And another angel came out of the temple which is in heaven, he also having a sharp sickle.

¹⁸And another angel came out from the altar, which had power over fire; and cried with a loud cry to him that had the sharp sickle, saying, Thrust in your sharp sickle, and gather the clusters of the vine of the earth; for her grapes are fully ripe.

¹⁹And the angel thrust in his sickle into the earth, and gathered the vine of the earth, and cast it into the great winepress of the wrath of God.

²⁰And the winepress was trodden outside the city, and blood came out of the winepress, even to the horse bridles, by the space of a thousand and six hundred furlongs.

given to the martyrs of this time. It is the choice of life and death.

Beginning in Revelation 14:14, we read of the great reaping of the earth's harvest. Christ comes with a sickle to harvest the earth. The living and the dead must be reaped. The reaping will be of the righteous and the wicked. In verses 15 and 16, we see the reaping of the righteous. This harvest is spoken of in Mark's gospel:

> But when the fruit is brought forth, immediately he puts in the sickle, because the harvest is come. (Mark 4:29)

The gold crown upon Christ's head in Revelation 14:14 was received in Revelation 6:2. At the firstfruits rapture, the overcoming saints will go, and the tribulation saints will be raptured later. With this great harvest rapture, the tribulation saints will be taken, and the sinners will be left to face the wrath of God.

In Revelation 14:17–20, we learn about how the vials will be poured out. Their final end will be the battle of Armageddon. (See Revelation 16:16.) The armies will mobilize at Armageddon, but the decisive battle will be outside Jerusalem. (See Revelation 14:20.) We will see God's wrath upon sin and upon sinners.

Revelation 14:19 speaks of *"the great winepress of the wrath of God."* The blood that results from this wrath reaches *"even to the horse bridles, by the space of a thousand and six hundred furlongs"* (Revelation 14:20). Sixteen hundred furlongs is about 170 miles. Compare this description of God's wrath with Isaiah's description:

> Who is this that comes from Edom, with dyed garments from Bozrah? this that is glorious in

His apparel, travelling in the greatness of His strength? I that speak in righteousness, mighty to save. Why are You red in Your apparel, and Your garments like him that treads in the winefat? I have trodden the winepress alone; and of the people there was none with Me: for I will tread them in My anger, and trample them in My fury; and their blood shall be sprinkled upon My garments, and I will stain all My raiment. For the day of vengeance is in My heart, and the year of My redeemed is come. And I looked, and there was none to help; and I wondered that there was none to uphold: therefore My own arm brought salvation to Me; and My fury, it upheld Me. And I will tread down the people in My anger, and make them drunk in My fury, and I will bring down their strength to the earth.

(Isaiah 63:1–6)

Look also at Ezekiel 39, Joel 3:9–16, and Zephaniah 1.

The outpouring of divine wrath will reach its peak at Armageddon. Evil spirits will lure the nations into that great battle. The destruction it causes will be so terrible that blood will flow for a distance of two hundred miles. The prophet Joel refers to this great gathering:

I will also gather all nations, and will bring them down into the valley of Jehoshaphat, and will plead with them there for My people and for My heritage Israel, whom they have scattered among the nations, and parted My land. (Joel 3:2)

CHAPTER FIFTEEN

Revelation 15 is the shortest chapter in Revelation. In it, we see the preparation for the last seven plagues. This chapter opens and closes with the wrath of God.

The parallel to this is in Revelation 8:1–6. The seven vials contain the fulfillment of God's wrath. When they are over, the millennium has arrived. The same thing was said of the seven trumpets. (See Revelation 11:15–19.)

The resurrection of the *"great multitude"* was reported in Revelation 7:9. Now we see them conducting a meeting in heaven. They are preparing to send out the seven last plagues. Please note that the nations are soon to come under the King of Kings.

How can those standing on the sea of glass (see verses 2–3) be so victorious when they are martyrs? The answer is in Corinthians:

O death, where is your sting? O grave, where is your victory? The sting of death is sin; and the strength of sin is the law. But thanks be to God, which gives us the victory through our Lord Jesus Christ. (1 Corinthians 15:55–57)

Martyrs receive crowns:

REVELATION 15

¹And I saw another sign in heaven, great and marvellous, seven angels having the seven last plagues; for in them is filled up the wrath of God.

²And I saw as it were a sea of glass mingled with fire: and them that had gotten the victory over the beast, and over his image, and over his mark, and over the number of his name, stand on the sea of glass, having the harps of God.

³And they sing the song of Moses the servant of God, and the song of the Lamb, saying, Great and marvellous are Your works, Lord God Almighty; just and true are Your ways, You King of saints.

⁴Who shall not fear You, O Lord, and glorify Your name? for You only are holy: for all nations shall come and worship before You; for Your judgments are made manifest.

NOTES

_____

_____

_____

_____

_____

_____

_____

_____

_____

REVELATION 15

⁵And after that I looked, and, behold, the temple of the tabernacle of the testimony in heaven was opened:

⁶and the seven angels came out of the temple, having the seven plagues, clothed in pure and white linen, and having their breasts girded with golden girdles.

⁷And one of the four beasts gave to the seven angels seven golden vials full of the wrath of God, who lives for ever and ever.

⁸And the temple was filled with smoke from the glory of God, and from His power; and no man was able to enter into the temple, till the seven plagues of the seven angels were fulfilled.

NOTES

_____

_____

_____

_____

_____

_____

_____

_____

_____

_____

_____

Blessed is the man that endures temptation: for when he is tried, he shall receive the crown of life, which the Lord has promised to them that love Him. (James 1:12)

Fear none of those things which you shall suffer: behold, the devil shall cast some of you into prison, that you may be tried; and you shall have tribulation ten days: be you faithful to death, and I will give you a crown of life. (Revelation 2:10)

These victorious ones have harps, and they sing the victorious song of Moses and the Lamb. Moses won over Pharaoh; God's people win over the Antichrist.

There are two songs of Moses: one in Exodus 15:1 and one in Deuteronomy 32. They are prophetic and apply to these judgments.

In Revelation 15:5–8, we have the pulling back of the curtain in heaven and the viewing of God's temple—it is awesome and judgmental. God commanded Moses to build a tabernacle after the pattern that is in heaven:

And let them make Me a sanctuary; that I may dwell among them. According to all that I show you, after the pattern of the tabernacle, and the pattern of all the instruments thereof, even so shall you make it. (Exodus 25:8–9)

Our fathers had the tabernacle of witness in the wilderness, as He had appointed, speaking to Moses, that he should make it according to the fashion that he had seen. (Acts 7:44)

Who serve to the example and shadow of heavenly things, as Moses was admonished of God when he was about to make the tabernacle: for,

*See, says He, that you make all things according
to the pattern showed to you in the mount.*
                                    (Hebrews 8:5)

Tabernacle means "holy of holies." The heavenly
temple contains the ark of the covenant:

*And the temple of God which is in heaven was
opened; and the ark of His covenant appeared in
His temple, and there were flashes of lightning
and sounds and peals of thunder and an earthquake and a great hailstorm.*
                          (Revelation 11:19 NASB)

The ark is a sign of victory for the saints, and a
sign of judgment for the sinner.

It seems strange that no man could enter the
temple until the seven last plagues were fulfilled. (See
verse 8.) This is because the temple is a place of intercession; there is to be no intercession, because wrath
is coming. The time of mercy is over; there is no stop-
ping the divine retribution about to begin.

CHAPTER SIXTEEN

NOTES

_____

_____

_____

_____

_____

_____

_____

_____

_____

_____

_____

_____

_____

_____

_____

_____

_____

Revelation 16 pictures Armageddon; this parallels Revelation 8–9. The new features are found in verses 12–16.

These vials are the trumpets of chapter eight. Compare the first trumpet and vial.

1

TRUMPET	VIAL
The first angel sounded, and there followed hail and fire mingled with blood, and they were cast upon the earth: and the third part of trees was burned up, and all green grass was burned up.	*And the first went, and poured out his vial upon the earth; and there fell a noisome and grievous sore upon the men which had the mark of the beast, and upon them which worshiped his image.*
(Revleation 8:7)	(Revelation 16:2)

These plagues have fire in them. It seems like the earth is on fire. It will bring an evil disease like was brought in Moses's day:

REVELATION 16

³And the second angel poured out his vial upon the sea; and it became as the blood of a dead man: and every living soul died in the sea.

NOTES

_____
_____
_____
_____
_____
_____
_____
_____
_____
_____
_____
_____
_____
_____
_____
_____
_____

And the magicians could not stand before Moses because of the boils; for the boil was upon the magicians, and upon all the Egyptians.

(Exodus 9:11)

The LORD will smite you with the botch of Egypt, and with the emerods and with the scab, and with the itch, whereof you can not be healed.

(Deuteronomy 28:27)

These cancerous sores on the worshippers of Antichrist are hideous. They are still there when we read about the fifth vial judgment.

Compare the second trumpet and vial:

2

TRUMPET	VIAL
And the second angel sounded, and as it were a great mountain burning with fire was cast into the sea: and the third part of the sea became blood; and the third part of the creatures which were in the sea, and had life, died; and the third part of the ships were destroyed. (Revleation 8:7)	And the second angel poured out his vial upon the sea; and it became as the blood of a dead man: and every living soul died in the sea. (Revelation 16:3)

This is a judgment on the sea. The beast came out of the sea in chapter 13. This vial judgment turns one-third of the sea into blood and kills animals and people. Their rotting bodies will fill every harbor.

This plague is also similar to one in Moses's day:

*And Moses and Aaron did so, as the L*ORD *commanded; and he lifted up the rod, and smote the waters that were in the river, in the sight of Pharaoh, and in the sight of his servants; and all the waters that were in the river were turned to blood. And the fish that was in the river died; and the river stunk, and the Egyptians could not drink of the water of the river; and there was blood throughout all the land of Egypt.*

(Exodus 7:20–21)

The third trumpet and vial:

3

TRUMPET	VIAL
And the third angel sounded, and there fell a great star from heaven, burning as it were a lamp, and it fell upon the third part of the rivers, and the name of the star is called Wormwood: and the third part of the waters became wormwood; and many men died of the waters, because they were made bitter. (Revelation 8:10–11)	*And the third angel poured out his vial upon the rivers and fountains of waters; and they became blood…. For they have shed the blood of saints and prophets, and You have given them blood to drink; for they are worthy.* (Revelation 16:4, 6)

Those who like to shed blood will now drink blood; it is the law of sowing and reaping in action.

The fourth trumpet and vial:

REVELATION 16

⁴And the third angel poured out his vial upon the rivers and fountains of waters; and they became blood.

⁵And I heard the angel of the waters say, You are righteous, O Lord, which are, and were, and shall be, because You have judged thus.

⁶For they have shed the blood of saints and prophets, and You have given them blood to drink; for they are worthy.

NOTES

_____

_____

_____

_____

_____

_____

_____

_____

_____

_____

_____

_____

_____

_____

_____

REVELATION 16

⁷And I heard another out of the altar say, Even so, Lord God Almighty, true and righteous are Your judgments.

⁸And the fourth angel poured out his vial upon the sun; and power was given to him to scorch men with fire.

⁹And men were scorched with great heat, and blasphemed the name of God, which has power over these plagues: and they repented not to give Him glory.

NOTES

_____

_____

_____

_____

_____

_____

_____

_____

_____

_____

_____

_____

4

TRUMPET	VIAL
And the fourth angel sounded, and the third part of the sun was smitten, and the third part of the moon, and the third part of the stars; so as the third part of them was darkened, and the day shone not for a third part of it, and the night likewise. (Revelation 8:12)	*And the fourth angel poured out his vial upon the sun; and power was given to him to scorch men with fire. And men were scorched with great heat, and blasphemed the name of God, which has power over these plagues: and they repented not to give Him glory.* (Revelation 16:8–9)

The power and heat of the sun are increased. Nature was perfectly balanced when God created the earth, but with man's fall, seasons moved out of balance:

> *They know not, neither will they understand; they walk on in darkness: all the foundations of the earth are out of course.* (Psalm 82:5)

This condition will be corrected during the millennium. The light of the sun will have its original strength:

> *Moreover the light of the moon shall be as the light of the sun, and the light of the sun shall be sevenfold, as the light of seven days, in the day that the LORD binds up the breach of His people, and heals the stroke of their wound.*
> (Isaiah 30:26)

When the earth was created, it was perfect. God said, *"It is good."* When man fell, so did creation:

The earth mourns and fades away, the world languishes and fades away, the haughty people of the earth do languish. The earth also is defiled under the inhabitants thereof; because they have transgressed the laws, changed the ordinance, broken the everlasting covenant. Therefore has the curse devoured the earth, and they that dwell therein are desolate: therefore the inhabitants of the earth are burned, and few men left.
(Isaiah 24:4–6)

For, behold, the day comes, that shall burn as an oven; and all the proud, yea, and all that do wickedly, shall be stubble: and the day that comes shall burn them up, says the Lord of hosts, that it shall leave them neither root nor branch.
(Malachi 4:1)

During the fourth trumpet/vial judgment, the sun is darkened one-third of the day and then becomes intensely hot. The first four plagues are against inanimate objects—earth, sea, rivers, and sun. God uses heat, fire, blood, wormwood, and darkness. The last three judgments will be against the beast, his kingdom, and his people.

The earth is full of germs, weeds, and pests of all kinds, and it must be cleansed to be returned to its original state. However, men do not repent. Men who sell themselves to the devil eventually become like the devil themselves.

The fifth trumpet and vial:

REVELATION 16

¹⁰And the fifth angel poured out his vial upon the seat of the beast; and his kingdom was full of darkness; and they gnawed their tongues for pain,

¹¹and blasphemed the God of heaven because of their pains and their sores, and repented not of their deeds.

NOTES

_____

_____

_____

_____

_____

_____

_____

_____

_____

_____

_____

_____

_____

_____

_____

_____

5

TRUMPET

And the fifth angel sounded, and I saw a star fall from heaven to the earth: and to him was given the key of the bottomless pit. And he opened the bottomless pit; and there arose a smoke out of the pit, as the smoke of a great furnace; and the sun and the air were darkened by reason of the smoke of the pit. And there came out of the smoke locusts upon the earth: and to them was given power, as the scorpions of the earth have power.

(Revelation 9:1–3)

VIAL

And the fifth angel poured out his vial upon the seat of the beast; and his kingdom was full of darkness; and they gnawed their tongues for pain, and blasphemed the God of heaven because of their pains and their sores, and repented not of their deeds.

(Revelation 9:1–3)

With their tongues, they blaspheme God, and now they punish their own tongues by gnawing on them. How terrible. This fifth vial is the plague of the hideous locusts. The poison stays in their bodies five months. The darkness of this plague is like the Egyptian plague:

And the Lord said to Moses, Stretch out your hand toward heaven, that there may be darkness over the land of Egypt, even darkness which may be felt. And Moses stretched forth his hand toward heaven; and there was a thick darkness

in all the land of Egypt three days: they saw not one another, neither rose any from his place for three days: but all the children of Israel had light in their dwellings. (Exodus 10:21–23)

The sixth plague brings forth the fallen angels.

6

TRUMPET

And the sixth angel sounded, and I heard a voice from the four horns of the golden altar which is before God, saying to the sixth angel which had the trumpet, Loose the four angels which are bound in the great river Euphrates. And the four angels were loosed, which were prepared for an hour, and a day, and a month, and a year, for to slay the third part of men. And the number of the army of the horsemen were two hundred thousand thousand: and I heard the number of them. And thus I saw the horses in the vision, and them that sat on them, having breastplates of fire, and of jacinth, and brimstone: and the heads of the horses were as the heads of lions; and out of their mouths issued fire and smoke and brimstone.

(Revelation 9:13–17)

VIAL

And the sixth angel poured out his vial upon the great river Euphrates; and the water thereof was dried up, that the way of the kings of the east might be prepared. And I saw three unclean spirits like frogs come out of the mouth of the dragon, and out of the mouth of the beast, and out of the mouth of the false prophet. For they are the spirits of devils, working miracles, which go forth to the kings of the earth and of the whole world, to gather them to the battle of that great day of God Almighty. Behold, I come as a thief. Blessed is he that watches, and keeps his garments, lest he walk naked, and they see his shame. And he gathered them together into a place called in the Hebrew tongue Armageddon.

(Revelation 16:12–16)

REVELATION 16

[12]And the sixth angel poured out his vial upon the great river Euphrates; and the water thereof was dried up, that the way of the kings of the east might be prepared.

[13]And I saw three unclean spirits like frogs come out of the mouth of the dragon, and out of the mouth of the beast, and out of the mouth of the false prophet.

[14]For they are the spirits of devils, working miracles, which go forth to the kings of the earth and of the whole world, to gather them to the battle of that great day of God Almighty.

[15]Behold, I come as a thief. Blessed is he that watches, and keeps his garments, lest he walk naked, and they see his shame.

[16]And he gathered them together into a place called in the Hebrew tongue Armageddon.

NOTES

_____

_____

_____

_____

_____

_____

_____

How tragic that the plagues bring no repentance.

In Revelation 16:13–14, we see three spirits that appear as frogs that proceed out of the satanic trinity. They are to gather the nations that are under the control of the Antichrist. In addition to this evil trinity, there is a fourth group, the kings of the east, which joins them to fight in the battle of Armageddon. The Euphrates will dry up in order for them to combine.

The river Euphrates refers to Babylon, the place where human rebellion began. It has always been the great dividing line between the east and the west. Genesis 15:18 mentions the Euphrates as a border to the lands promised to Israel. Here in Revelation 16, we see that geographical hindrances will hold back these armies of the east. However, east and west will eventually meet. Evil, lying spirits will seduce them as in Ahab's day:

And he said, Hear you therefore the word of the Lord: I saw the Lord sitting on His throne, and all the host of heaven standing by Him on His right hand and on His left. And the Lord said, Who shall persuade Ahab, that he may go up and fall at Ramothgilead? And one said on this manner, and another said on that manner. And there came forth a spirit, and stood before the Lord, and said, I will persuade him. And the Lord said to him, Wherewith? And he said, I will go forth, and I will be a lying spirit in the mouth of all his prophets. And He said, You shall persuade him, and prevail also: go forth, and do so. Now therefore, behold, the Lord has put a lying spirit in the mouth of all these your prophets, and the Lord has spoken evil concerning you. (1 Kings 22:19–23)

Ezekiel 38 and 39 give this account also. There are four groups of nations. Three of them are under the Antichrist and independent. The first are Meshech and Tubal; the second are Persia, Ethiopia, and Libya; and the third are Gomer (possibly today's Dahube and Rhine valleys) and Togarmah (today's Armenia). Communism and the Antichrist will come together for a season for an uneasy partnership. However, they will clash at Armageddon.

The second group—Persia, Ethiopia, and Libya—are named because they are the same today as in Ezekiel's day. The others are grandsons of Noah, who, in a general way, inhabited the countries of which Ezekiel talks. Gomer and Togarmah are the nations of Europe. Meshech and Tubal are north of Palestine and probably part of southern Russia, near the Black and Caspian Seas.

The fourth group of nations are independent, and the first to descend upon Israel when invasion is threatened:

Sheba, and Dedan, and the merchants of Tarshish, with all the young lions thereof, shall say to you, Are you come to take a spoil? have you gathered your company to take a prey? to carry away silver and gold, to take away cattle and goods, to take a great spoil? (Ezekiel 38:13)

The names Sheba and Dedan are not important today, but as they are within modern day Arabia they are very important. The merchants of Tarshish are Gibraltar, (the Mediterranean) and the young lions could be the offshoots of Great Britain, such as America, Canada, and Australia. These come to hinder the Antichrist.

The sixth and seventh vials, remember, correspond to the sixth and seventh trumpets. Satan always tries to counterfeit what God does; just like the Egyptians tried to duplicate the plagues by Moses. When the two witnesses are sent to work miracles, Satan also sends out evil spirits to work miracles. Eventually, the two witnesses are killed. Then Satan closes in, and we begin to see Armageddon forming:

And He will lift up an ensign to the nations from far, and will hiss to them from the end of the earth: and, behold, they shall come with speed swiftly: none shall be weary nor stumble among them; none shall slumber nor sleep; neither shall the girdle of their loins be loosed, nor the latchet of their shoes be broken: whose arrows are sharp, and all their bows bent, their horses' hoofs shall be counted like flint, and their wheels like a whirlwind: their roaring shall be like a lion, they shall roar like young lions: yea, they shall roar, and lay hold of the prey, and shall carry it away safe, and none shall deliver it. And in that day they shall roar against them like the roaring of the sea: and if one look to the land, behold darkness and sorrow, and the light is darkened in the heavens thereof. (Isaiah 5:26–30)

Armageddon is more than an ordinary war. It is a war against God. The rulers of the earth, filled with madness, will try to dethrone God:

The kings of the earth set themselves, and the rulers take counsel together, against the Lord, and against His Anointed, saying, Let us break their bands asunder, and cast away their cords from us. He that sits in the heavens shall laugh: the Lord shall have them in derision. (Psalm 2:2–4)

Armageddon is an ancient gathering place for armies.

Compare the seventh trumpet and vial judgments:

7

TRUMPET

And the seventh angel sounded; and there were great voices in heaven, saying, The kingdoms of this world are become the kingdoms of our Lord, and of His Christ; and He shall reign for ever and ever. And the four and twenty elders, which sat before God on their seats, fell upon their faces, and worshiped God, saying, We give You thanks, O Lord God Almighty, which are, and were, and are to come; because You have taken to You Your great power, and have reigned. And the nations were angry, and Your wrath is come, and the time of the dead, that they should be judged, and that You should give reward to Your servants the prophets, and to the saints, and them that fear Your name, small and great; and should destroy them which destroy the earth. And the temple of God was opened in heaven, and there was seen in His temple the ark of His testament: and there were lightnings, and voices, and thunderings, and an earthquake, and great hail.

(Revelation 11:15–19)

VIAL

And the seventh angel poured out his vial into the air; and there came a great voice out of the temple of heaven, from the throne, saying, It is done. And there were voices, and thunders, and lightnings; and there was a great earthquake, such as was not since men were upon the earth, so mighty an earthquake, and so great. And the great city was divided into three parts, and the cities of the nations fell: and great Babylon came in remembrance before God, to give to her the cup of the wine of the fierceness of His wrath. And every island fled away, and the mountains were not found. And there fell upon men a great hail out of heaven, every stone about the weight of a talent: and men blasphemed God because of the plague of the hail; for the plague thereof was exceeding great.

(Revelation 16:17–21)

REVELATION 16

¹⁷And the seventh angel poured out his vial into the air; and there came a great voice out of the temple of heaven, from the throne, saying, It is done.

¹⁸And there were voices, and thunders, and lightnings; and there was a great earthquake, such as was not since men were upon the earth, so mighty an earthquake, and so great.

¹⁹And the great city was divided into three parts, and the cities of the nations fell: and great Babylon came in remembrance before God, to give to her the cup of the wine of the fierceness of His wrath.

²⁰And every island fled away, and the mountains were not found.

²¹And there fell upon men a great hail out of heaven, every stone about the weight of a talent: and men blasphemed God because of the plague of the hail; for the plague thereof was exceeding great.

NOTES

_____

_____

_____

_____

_____

_____

_____

_____

Now we have only a war and an earthquake to come. The earthquake of this seventh vial judgment will be the greatest in all of history. The earthquake shakes the earth before the last battle. Isaiah describes it:

The earth shall reel to and fro like a drunkard, and shall be removed like a cottage; and the transgression thereof shall be heavy upon it; and it shall fall, and not rise again. (Isaiah 24:20)

The earthquake will make the earth level, as it was originally before the flood. Great hail weighing sixty pounds will fall. Mountains will move. The topography will dramatically change. However, the Antichrist (iron) and the clay of human government will not adhere, and Armageddon will "backlash" upon them because God is still in control.

Let's do a review of this seventh trumpet/vial judgment:

1. The atmosphere changes with thunders and lightnings.

2. There is the greatest earthquake.

3. Jerusalem is divided into three parts by the earthquake.

4. Cities fall.

5. There is great hail from heaven.

6. Babylon receives the cup of God's wrath.

ARMAGEDDON

End-time prophecies are being fulfilled every day. The news tells us about wars and rumors of war, as well as strife, plague, famine, pestilence, and natural disasters. Reports abound that Christians all over the world are hated, tortured, killed, taken to court, and betrayed by family members. Newscasts tell us of false prophets who are leading many astray. Crime and lawlessness abound. Parents are killing their children. Even children are killing other children.

Our world seems to be going mad! Every day, the devil gains new ground, claiming the hearts and minds of individuals, families, and nations. Despite all this, I am not afraid. I am encouraged, because two thousand years ago, Jesus told us that these things would come to pass in the last days. Each war, famine, plague, and disaster are reminders that God's plan and purpose for this world are being fulfilled exactly as prophesied.

THE FINAL CURTAIN?

The entire subject of the end times is shrouded with mystery and centuries of heated theological debate, but no aspect of the end times is as misunderstood as Armageddon.

The word strikes fear into the hearts of some, but to others, the word *Armageddon* has become nothing more than a term signifying the struggle between good and evil, a bloody war without winners, or the end of mankind.

Armageddon *is* a terrible battle that will create a river of blood. It is the final rebellion of Satan and man against God. The Antichrist will gather a global army in Israel and ravage the land on his way to Jerusalem, pillaging cities and killing thousands.

However, not once do Satan and his servants lift a sword against the Lord. When Christ returns with His bride to earth, Satan's army is destroyed by the voice of our Savior. (See Joel 2:11.) Therefore, there is no real *struggle* between good and evil, because Christ overcomes without lifting a finger.

There *are* winners at Armageddon! God's righteous—Christians and all the Jews who believe in their Messiah—will receive the title deed to earth. They will live without evil in their midst. They will be part of the divine process of restoring this world into the paradise it was before man's fall from grace.

Armageddon does not mark the end of mankind. In bodies that don't die and with hearts that don't break, mankind begins an eternity of praise and fellowship with our Father, our Savior, the Holy Spirit, and our brethren in Christ.

ARMAGEDDON

The word *Armageddon* appears only once in the Bible: *"For they are spirits of devils, working miracles, which go forth to the kings of the earth and of the whole world, to gather them to the battle of that great day of God Almighty…. And he gathered them together into a place called in the Hebrew tongue, Armageddon"* (Revelation 16:14, 16). Throughout the Bible, this valley is called by other names, including the Valley of Megiddo and the Valley of Jezreel.

Armageddon means "hill of Megiddo" in Hebrew. I've visited Megiddo countless times, and I always find the area awesome as I look down from the ruins of King Solomon's once-magnificent horse stables into the Valley of Jezreel, which is what the Israelis call the area today.

The Valley of Jezreel is fertile and lush, with grapes, barley, and potatoes growing there in abundance. The nation of Israel is fed with these crops. It is a calm place, where the morning sunshine chases away the mists of the Kishon River Valley.

It's hard to believe that this serene setting has been the site of countless battles in history, and that it will be the gathering place for Satan's monstrous army at the end of the tribulation.

ARMAGEDDON IN HISTORY

In Hebrew, the word *Megiddo* means "assembly, rendezvous." It is derived from *gradad*, which means "to crowd, assemble by troops." Its name is well suited. This valley, fifty-five miles northwest of Jerusalem, was the crossroads of two ancient trade routes: one leading from the Mediterranean Sea on the west to the Jordan River on the east; and the other leading from Syria, Phoenicia, and Galilee in the north to the hill country of Judah and the land of Egypt on the south. It has been a strategic military site and the scene of numerous ancient battles, many of which were fought by the people of Israel.

The king of Megiddo was one of thirty-one Canaanite kings whom Joshua and the Israelites conquered in order to claim the Promised Land. (See Joshua 12:21.) The land then became the possession of the tribe of Manasseh, but the people were afraid to drive out the Canaanites who lived there, because they had chariots of iron. (See Joshua 17:12–18.)

Ahaziah, king of Judah, was attacked on the way to Gur when he fled Jehu and then died in Megiddo (see 2 Kings 9:27); and all the people associated with King Ahab's reign, including Jezebel, were assassinated by the followers of Jehu in the Valley of Jezreel. (See

2 Kings 9–10.) The Philistines were victorious over King Saul there (see 1 Samuel 31:1–3), and the Egyptians mortally wounded Josiah, king of Judah, when he attempted to intercept the army of Pharaoh Necho in the valley (see 2 Kings 23:29).

During the period of the judges, the forces of Deborah and Barak wiped out the army of Sisera in the swampy riverbanks of the Kishon River (see Judges 4) and the kings of Canaan who fought against Israel for repression of the land were defeated in Taanach on the river's edge (see Judges 5:19).

The world's final battle, the Battle of Armageddon, begins in this valley, but it isn't fought there. Megiddo is only the gathering place. Once assembled there, the Antichrist's demon-powered army marches in absolute precision down the Valley of Jezreel to the Jordan River valley, and then they head south. They turn west near Jericho and head to Jerusalem, where the final battle takes place. This is the Valley of Jehoshaphat.

THE END TIMES

As you study Armageddon, and the events leading up to it, it's important to understand that you won't know exactly when the rapture will occur, nor will anyone be able to definitely say who the Antichrist is.

God told us that humans only *"know in part"* (1 Corinthians 13:9), because prophecy is a mirror we can only see into dimly. (See 1 Corinthians 13:12.) Although the prophecies seem difficult, when you compare Scripture with Scripture, you can see the details unfolding, and the full scope of the prophecy taking shape. And each day, as we come closer to Christ's return, new events are revealed that help us understand the things He has shown us in prophesies, dreams, and visions.

When that which is perfect is come, then that which is in part shall be done away.
(1 Corinthians 13:10)

CHAPTER SEVENTEEN

Chapters 17 and 18 of Revelation reveal the doom of Babylon. Satan has always had a false religion. All the false religions will come under one umbrella during the tribulation.

The woman arrayed in scarlet is the counterfeit of the woman clothed with the sun in Revelation 12:

1. Both women have children. The woman of Revelation 12 had a man child, and the woman of chapter 17 was the mother of harlots and abominations.

2. Both women have power and influence. One woman has the moon under her feet and wears a crown of twelve stars, while the other woman has a beast beneath her with seven heads.

3. The women have different enemies: the dragon stands before the woman of chapter 12 to destroy her man child; ten kings of the beast eventually hate the woman of chapter 17 and are ready to burn her flesh with fire:

And the ten horns which you saw upon the beast,
these shall hate the whore, and shall make her

REVELATION 17

[1]And there came one of the seven angels which had the seven vials, and talked with me, saying to me, Come here; I will show to you the judgment of the great whore that sits upon many waters:

[2]with whom the kings of the earth have committed fornication, and the inhabitants of the earth have been made drunk with the wine of her fornication.

[3]So he carried me away in the Spirit into the wilderness: and I saw a woman sit upon a scarlet colored beast, full of names of blasphemy, having seven heads and ten horns.

[4]And the woman was arrayed in purple and scarlet color, and decked with gold and precious stones and pearls, having a golden cup in her hand full of abominations and filthiness of her fornication:

[5]And upon her forehead was a name written, MYSTERY, BABYLON THE GREAT, THE MOTHER OF HARLOTS AND ABOMINATIONS OF THE EARTH.

[6]And I saw the woman drunken with the blood of the saints, and with the blood of the martyrs of Jesus: and when I saw her, I wondered with great admiration.

[7]And the angel said to me, Wherefore did you marvel? I will tell you the mystery of the woman, and of the beast that carries her, which has the seven heads and ten horns.

⁸The beast that you saw was, and is not; and shall ascend out of the bottomless pit, and go into perdition: and they that dwell on the earth shall wonder, whose names were not written in the book of life from the foundation of the world, when they behold the beast that was, and is not, and yet is.

⁹And here is the mind which has wisdom. The seven heads are seven mountains, on which the woman sits.

¹⁰And there are seven kings: five are fallen, and one is, and the other is not yet come; and when he comes, he must continue a short space.

¹¹And the beast that was, and is not, even he is the eighth, and is of the seven, and goes into perdition.

¹²And the ten horns which you saw are ten kings, which have received no kingdom as yet; but receive power as kings one hour with the beast.

¹³These have one mind, and shall give their power and strength to the beast.

¹⁴These shall make war with the Lamb, and the Lamb shall overcome them: for He is Lord of lords, and King of kings: and they that are with Him are called, and chosen, and faithful.

¹⁵And he says to me, The waters which you saw, where the whore sits, are peoples, and multitudes, and nations, and tongues.

¹⁶And the ten horns which you saw upon the beast, these shall hate the *desolate and naked, and shall eat her flesh, and burn her with fire.* (Revelation 17:16)

4.   The woman of chapter 12 will enter the new Jerusalem and make it her home for all eternity. The woman of chapter 17 will go into perdition.

The woman of chapter 17 sits upon the beast, which fits the description of the Antichrist. We have seen the struggle of power between the Holy Trinity (Father, Son, and Holy Spirit) and the *unholy* trinity (devil, Antichrist, and false prophet). There is also the struggle between the true and false churches.

The false church will sit on top of the end-time nations. Historically, the false church began with the building of Babel by Nimrod. It started in sin:

And Cush fathered Nimrod: he began to be a mighty one in the earth. He was a mighty hunter before the LORD: wherefore it is said, Even as Nimrod the mighty hunter before the LORD. And the beginning of his kingdom was Babel, and Erech, and Accad, and Calneh, in the land of Shinar. (Genesis 10:8–10)

The purpose for building the tower of Babel was to make a name for the builders. They tried to begin a new and idolatrous religion. *Babel* means "gate of God." God confused their tongues and scattered them. Paul refers to them in the book of Romans:

Because that, when they knew God, they glorified Him not as God, neither were thankful; but became vain in their imaginations, and their foolish heart was darkened. Professing themselves to be wise, they became fools, and changed the glory of the incorruptible God into an image made like to corruptible man, and to birds, and four-footed beasts, and creeping things…. And even as they did not like to retain God in their knowledge, God gave them over to a reprobate mind, to do those things which are not convenient.

(Romans 1:21–23, 28)

Abraham was called out of the Babylonian area:

And Joshua said to all the people, Thus says the LORD *God of Israel, Your fathers dwelled on the other side of the flood in old time, even Terah, the father of Abraham, and the father of Nachor: and they served other gods.* (Joshua 24:2)

Achan stole a Babylonian garment and was stoned to death:

And Achan answered Joshua, and said, Indeed I have sinned against the LORD *God of Israel, and thus and thus have I done: when I saw among the spoils a goodly Babylonish garment, and two hundred shekels of silver, and a wedge of gold of fifty shekels weight, then I coveted them, and took them; and, behold, they are hidden in the earth in the midst of my tent, and the silver under it.* (Joshua 7:20–21)

When Israel fell into idolatry, they were carried away to Babylon. Nebuchadnezzar made a golden image to worship. His grandson profaned the vessels of the house of God. Babylon was judged and passed into the hands of Darius the Mede.

"MYSTERY, BABYLON" (Revelation 17:5) represents false religion, which has been here through the ages. It is Satan's substitute for true Christianity.

In Revelation 17:1, the woman is seen sitting *"upon many waters."* This means that she has many people under her power:

whore, and shall make her desolate and naked, and shall eat her flesh, and burn her with fire.

[17]For God has put in their hearts to fulfill His will, and to agree, and give their kingdom to the beast, until the words of God shall be fulfilled.

[18]And the woman which you saw is that great city, which reigns over the kings of the earth.

NOTES

_____

_____

_____

_____

_____

_____

_____

_____

_____

_____

_____

_____

_____

_____

_____

_____
_____
_____
_____
_____
_____
_____
_____
_____
_____
_____
_____
_____
_____
_____
_____
_____
_____
_____
_____
_____
_____
_____
_____

And he says to me, The waters which you saw, where the whore sits, are peoples, and multitudes, and nations, and tongues. (Revelation 17:15)

The beast of Revelation 17:8 is the devil. He comes out of the bottomless pit and goes into perdition. He is the prince of the world.

The seven mountains in Revelation 17:9–10 refer to the seven kings, or seven world empires. Five are fallen: Egypt, Assyria, Babylon, Persia, and Greece. One empire *"is,"* which, of course, is the Roman Empire during John's time, and the other, which is *"not yet come,"* is the empire ruled by the Antichrist in the last days. He is called the eighth, but he came out of the seventh:

And the beast that was, and is not, even he is the eighth, and is of the seven, and goes into perdition. (Revelation 17:11)

At the time of the rapture, Satan will take over an empire, arrange the world into ten kingdoms, and extend the Antichrist's power to the world. The beast will set his kings over these nations, but their reign will be short, as indicated by the term *"one hour"*:

And the ten horns which you saw are ten kings, which have received no kingdom as yet; but receive power as kings one hour with the beast. (Revelation 17:12)

The war with the Lamb, mentioned in Revelation 17:14, is the battle of Armageddon described in chapter 19.

The Antichrist will be the harvest of modernism, which is humanism—the worship of man and, finally, the worship of *a* man. Humanism has always been the devil's tool.

CHAPTER EIGHTEEN

Revelation 18:2 speaks of a great city, and yet we have seen Babylon destroyed in Revelation 17. Most Bible scholars believe that *"MYSTERY, BABYLON,"* the religious system, is destroyed in chapter 17. Chapter 18 is concerned with *commercial* Babylon.

A natural Babylon will be built on the base of the old. It will be a commercial center. It will have a religious system behind it, as well as a commercial system. Jeremiah warned about it:

And I will punish Bel in Babylon, and I will bring forth out of his mouth that which he has swallowed up: and the nations shall not flow together any more to him: yea, the wall of Babylon shall fall. (Jeremiah 51:44)

In the days of Nebuchadnezzar, Babylon was one of the seven ancient wonders of the world. Its capture by Cyrus in the sixth century was predicted by Isaiah one hundred twenty-five years before it happened:

That says of Cyrus, he is My shepherd, and shall perform all My pleasure: even saying to Jerusalem, You shall be built; and to the temple, Your foundation shall be laid. (Isaiah 44:28)

REVELATION 18

¹And after these things I saw another angel come down from heaven, having great power; and the earth was lightened with his glory.

²And he cried mightily with a strong voice, saying, Babylon the great is fallen, is fallen, and is become the habitation of devils, and the hold of every foul spirit, and a cage of every unclean and hateful bird.

³For all nations have drunk of the wine of the wrath of her fornication, and the kings of the earth have committed fornication with her, and the merchants of the earth are waxed rich through the abundance of her delicacies.

⁴And I heard another voice from heaven, saying, Come out of her, my people, that you be not partakers of her sins, and that you receive not of her plagues.

⁵For her sins have reached to heaven, and God has remembered her iniquities.

⁶Reward her even as she rewarded you, and double to her double according to her works: in the cup which she has filled fill to her double.

⁷How much she has glorified herself, and lived deliciously, so much torment and sorrow give her: for she says in her heart, I sit a queen, and am no widow, and shall see no sorrow.

⁸Therefore shall her plagues come in one day, death, and mourning, and famine; and she shall be utterly burned with fire: for strong is the Lord God who judges her.

⁹And the kings of the earth, who have committed fornication and lived deliciously with her, shall bewail her, and lament for her, when they shall see the smoke of her burning,

¹⁰standing afar off for the fear of her torment, saying, Alas, alas, that great city Babylon, that mighty city! for in one hour is your judgment come.

¹¹And the merchants of the earth shall weep and mourn over her; for no man buys their merchandise any more:

¹²the merchandise of gold, and silver, and precious stones, and of pearls, and fine linen, and purple, and silk, and scarlet, and all thyine wood, and all manner vessels of ivory, and all manner vessels of most precious wood, and of brass, and iron, and marble,

¹³and cinnamon, and odors, and ointments, and frankincense, and wine, and oil, and fine flour, and wheat, and beasts, and sheep, and horses, and chariots, and slaves, and souls of men.

¹⁴And the fruits that your soul lusted after are departed from you, and all things which were dainty and goodly are departed from you, and you shall find them no more at all.

Thus says the Lord *to His anointed, to Cyrus, whose right hand I have held, to subdue nations before him; and I will loose the loins of kings, to open before him the two leaved gates; and the gates shall not be shut; I will go before you, and make the crooked places straight: I will break in pieces the gates of brass, and cut in sunder the bars of iron.* (Isaiah 45:1–2)

This was when a hand wrote on the wall, telling King Belshazzar that he'd been weighed in the balances and found wanting. (See Daniel 5.) The result of this would be the division of his kingdom between the Medes and Persians. The Medes were clever. They diverted the river that went through that city. Then they entered on dry land beneath the gates and took the city. It would have been impossible had not God given the Medes and the Persians the plan. From that time on, Babylon began to decline, until a thousand years later, it was only a small village.

Isaiah prophesied of this fall:

And Babylon, the glory of kingdoms, the beauty of the Chaldees' excellency, shall be as when God overthrew Sodom and Gomorrah. It shall never be inhabited, neither shall it be dwelled in from generation to generation: neither shall the Arabian pitch tent there; neither shall the shepherds make their fold there. But wild beasts of the desert shall lie there; and their houses shall be full of doleful creatures; and owls shall dwell there, and satyrs shall dance there. And the wild beasts of the islands shall cry in their desolate houses, and dragons in their pleasant palaces: and her time is near to come, and her days shall not be prolonged. (Isaiah 13:19–22)

After Babylon fell to the Medes, it began to go downhill. A century later, Alexander the Great conquered it. Then a rival city sprang up and drew off many of its inhabitants. Babylon was a city in the day of the apostle Peter; he wrote an epistle from there:

The church that is at Babylon, elected together with you, salutes you; and so does Marcus my son. (1 Peter 5:13)

A thousand years later, Babylon was only a small village. It is now totally deserted.

However, in Isaiah 13, there is a special judgment on Babylon at the end of the age:

Howl you; for the day of the LORD is at hand; it shall come as a destruction from the Almighty.... Behold, the day of the LORD come, cruel both with wrath and fierce anger, to lay the land desolate: and He shall destroy the sinners thereof out of it. For the stars of heaven and the constellations thereof shall not give their light: the sun shall be darkened in its going forth, and the moon shall not cause her light to shine. (Isaiah 13:6, 9–10)

That is why many scholars believe that Babylon will be rebuilt. Jeremiah also prophesied a judgment upon this Babylon at the end of the age:

And Babylon shall become heaps, a dwelling-place for dragons, an astonishment, and a hissing, without an inhabitant. (Jeremiah 51:37)

How is Sheshach taken! and how is the praise of the whole earth surprised! how is Babylon become an astonishment among the nations! The sea is come up upon Babylon: she is covered with the multitude of the waves thereof. Her cities

[15]The merchants of these things, which were made rich by her, shall stand afar off for the fear of her torment, weeping and wailing,

[16]and saying, Alas, alas, that great city, that was clothed in fine linen, and purple, and scarlet, and decked with gold, and precious stones, and pearls!

[17]For in one hour so great riches is come to nothing. And every shipmaster, and all the company in ships, and sailors, and as many as trade by sea, stood afar off,

[18]and cried when they saw the smoke of her burning, saying, what city is like to this great city!

[19]And they cast dust on their heads, and cried, weeping and wailing, saying, Alas, alas, that great city, wherein were made rich all that had ships in the sea by reason of her costliness! for in one hour is she made desolate.

[20]Rejoice over her, you heaven, and you holy apostles and prophets; for God has avenged you on her.

[21]And a mighty angel took up a stone like a great millstone, and cast it into the sea, saying, Thus with violence shall that great city Babylon be thrown down, and shall be found no more at all.

[22]And the voice of harpers, and musicians, and of pipers, and trumpeters, shall be heard no more at all in you; and no craftsman, of whatsoever craft he be, shall be found any more in you; and the sound of

a millstone shall be heard no more at all in you;

23and the light of a candle shall shine no more at all in you; and the voice of the bridegroom and of the bride shall be heard no more at all in you: for your merchants were the great men of the earth; for by your sorceries were all nations deceived.

24And in her was found the blood of prophets, and of saints, and of all that were slain upon the earth.

NOTES

_____

_____

_____

_____

_____

_____

_____

_____

_____

_____

_____

_____

_____

_____

_____

are a desolation, a dry land, and a wilderness, a land wherein no man dwells, neither does any son of man pass thereby. And I will punish Bel in Babylon, and I will bring forth out of his mouth that which he has swallowed up: and the nations shall not flow together any more to him: yea, the wall of Babylon shall fall. My people, go you out of the midst of her, and deliver you every man his soul from the fierce anger of the Lord.... As Babylon has caused the slain of Israel to fall, so at Babylon shall fall the slain of all the earth.

(Jeremiah 51:41–45, 49)

Though Babylon should mount up to heaven, and though she should fortify the height of her strength, yet from Me shall spoilers come to her, says the Lord.... Thus says the Lord of hosts; The broad walls of Babylon shall be utterly broken, and her high gates shall be burned with fire; and the people shall labor in vain, and the folk in the fire, and they shall be weary.... Then shall you say, O Lord, you have spoken against this place, to cut it off, that none shall remain in it, neither man nor beast, but that it shall be desolate for ever. And it shall be, when you have made an end of reading this book, that you shall bind a stone to it, and cast it into the midst of Euphrates: and you shall say, Thus shall Babylon sink, and shall not rise from the evil that I will bring upon her: and they shall be weary. Thus far are the words of Jeremiah.

(Jeremiah 51:53, 58, 62–64)

There definitely appears to be a judgment on Babylon at the end of the age. It appears that the Antichrist will rebuild Babylon, which will be destroyed at the judgments of the day of the Lord.

With the current events surrounding Iran and Iraq, these prophecies appear even closer than five years ago.

Zechariah has an unusual description of Babylon being rebuilt:

> *And he said to me, To build it a house in the land of Shinar: and it shall be established, and set there upon her own base.* (Zechariah 5:11)

The *"land of Shinar,"* of course, is another word for Babylon. These two words could represent the two Babylons—the religious and the commercial. God calls His people to come out of her:

> *And I heard another voice from heaven, saying, Come out of her, my people, that you be not partakers of her sins, and that you receive not of her plagues.* (Revelation 18:4)

In Zechariah 5:9–11, the prophet gives an account of two women with an ephah. *Ephah* is a commercial measure. The women are moving their location to Shinar, the land of Babylon. They are moving to a new base of operation.

In Revelation 18:8–10, we see a tremendous burning of the city. It could be something like the fire from heaven that fell upon Sodom and Gomorrah, or it could also be a nuclear bomb. Babylon once burned the city of Jerusalem; now she shall be destroyed by *fire:*

> *And Babylon, the glory of kingdoms, the beauty of the Chaldees' excellency, shall be as when God overthrew Sodom and Gomorrah.* (Isaiah 13:19)

And I will render to Babylon and to all the inhabitants of Chaldea all their evil that they have done in Zion in your sight, says the LORD.
(Jeremiah 51:24)

This certainly ties in with Revelation 18:6:

Reward her even as she rewarded you, and double to her double according to her works: in the cup which she has filled fill to her double.

Commercial Babylon will be built quickly and will fall quickly. The message to us today: "Don't let your heart become covetous!"

CHAPTER NINETEEN

John sees a great multitude in heaven, celebrating God's judgment on Babylon. This was predicted by Jeremiah:

> Then the heaven and the earth, and all that is therein, shall sing for Babylon: for the spoilers shall come to her from the north, says the LORD.
> (Jeremiah 51:48)

Chapter 19 of Revelation parallels the activities of the seventh trumpet recorded in Revelation 11:

> And the seventh angel sounded; and there were great voices in heaven, saying, The kingdoms of this world are become the kingdoms of our Lord, and of His Christ; and He shall reign for ever and ever. And the four and twenty elders, which sat before God on their seats, fell upon their faces, and worshiped God, saying, We give You thanks, O Lord God Almighty, which are, and were, and are to come; because You have taken to You Your great power, and have reigned. And the nations were angry, and Your wrath is come, and the time of the dead, that they should be judged, and that You should give reward to Your

REVELATION 19

¹And after these things I heard a great voice of many people in heaven, saying, Alleluia; Salvation, and glory, and honor, and power, to the Lord our God:

²for true and righteous are His judgments: for He has judged the great whore, which did corrupt the earth with her fornication, and has avenged the blood of His servants at her hand.

³And again they said, Alleluia. And her smoke rose up for ever and ever.

⁴And the four and twenty elders and the four beasts fell down and worshiped God that sat on the throne, saying, Amen; Alleluia.

⁵And a voice came out of the throne, saying, Praise our God, all you His servants, and you that fear Him, both small and great.

⁶And I heard as it were the voice of a great multitude, and as the voice of many waters, and as the voice of mighty thunderings, saying, Alleluia: for the Lord God omnipotent reigns.

⁷Let us be glad and rejoice, and give honor to Him: for the marriage of the Lamb is come, and His wife has made herself ready.

⁸And to her was granted that she should be arrayed in fine linen, clean and white: for the fine linen is the righteousness of saints.

⁹And he says to me, Write, Blessed are they which are called to the marriage supper of the Lamb. And

he says to me, These are the true sayings of God.

¹⁰And I fell at his feet to worship him. And he said to me, See you do it not: I am your fellow-servant, and of your brethren that have the testimony of Jesus: worship God: for the testimony of Jesus is the spirit of prophecy.

NOTES

_____

_____

_____

_____

_____

_____

_____

_____

_____

_____

_____

_____

_____

_____

_____

_____

_____

_____

servants the prophets, and to the saints, and them that fear Your name, small and great; and should destroy them which destroy the earth.
(Revelation 11:15–18)

Prior to Christ's physical return with the saints to earth to *"smite the nations"* (Revelation 19:15), there is the glorious *"marriage supper of the Lamb"* (verse 9). Here we see the oneness of Christ and His church, which Paul described:

For this cause shall a man leave his father and mother, and shall be joined to his wife, and they two shall be one flesh. This is a great mystery: but I speak concerning Christ and the church.
(Ephesians 5:31–32)

This marriage supper was spoken of by Jesus in Matthew 22:1–14:

The kingdom of heaven is like to a certain king, which made a marriage for his son.
(Matthew 22:2)

It is important to keep in mind the two parts of the second coming of Christ. First, there is the coming of Christ *for* His church (the rapture) at the start of the tribulation period. This will be followed at the *end* of the tribulation by the coming of Christ *with* His church, as described beginning in Revelation 19:11. It is this second aspect of the Second Coming that is spoken of in Acts:

Which also said, You men of Galilee, why stand you gazing up into heaven? this same Jesus, which is taken up from you into heaven, shall so come in like manner as you have seen Him go into heaven. (Acts 1:11)

Psalms 45 looks forward to the marriage of the Lamb and His bride, and also foretells of Christ's return to earth to set up His kingdom:

And in Your majesty ride prosperously because of truth and meekness and righteousness; and Your right hand shall teach You terrible things. Your arrows are sharp in the heart of the king's enemies; whereby the people fall under You…. So shall the king greatly desire your beauty: for He is your Lord; and worship you Him.
(Psalm 45:4–5, 11)

Out of Christ's mouth will go a sharp sword:

And out of His mouth goes a sharp sword, that with it He should smite the nations: and He shall rule them with a rod of iron: and He treads the winepress of the fierceness and wrath of Almighty God. (Revelation 19:15)

But with righteousness shall He judge the poor, and reprove with equity for the meek of the earth: and He shall smite the earth with the rod of His mouth, and with the breath of His lips shall He slay the wicked. (Isaiah 11:4)

As soon then as He had said to them, I am He, they went backward, and fell to the ground.
(John 18:6)

For the word of God is quick, and powerful, and sharper than any two-edged sword, piercing even to the dividing asunder of soul and spirit, and of the joints and marrow, and is a discerner of the thoughts and intents of the heart.
(Hebrews 4:12)

REVELATION 19

¹¹And I saw heaven opened, and behold a white horse; and He that sat upon him was called Faithful and True, and in righteousness He does judge and make war.

¹²His eyes were as a flame of fire, and on His head were many crowns; and He had a name written, that no man knew, but He Himself.

¹³And He was clothed with a vesture dipped in blood: and His name is called The Word of God.

¹⁴And the armies which were in heaven followed Him upon white horses, clothed in fine linen, white and clean.

¹⁵And out of His mouth goes a sharp sword, that with it He should smite the nations: and He shall rule them with a rod of iron: and He treads the winepress of the fierceness and wrath of Almighty God.

¹⁶And He has on His vesture and on His thigh a name written, KING OF KINGS, AND LORD OF LORDS.

NOTES

_____

_____

_____

_____

_____

_____

In Revelation 19:16, Jesus is seen as King of Kings and Lord of Lords. Please remember that Christ was to come of David's seed, and David's throne was to never end. Christ's kingdom is of David's kingdom, and David was a very prominent forerunner of Jesus Christ.

There were three anointings of David to be the king. His first anointing to be king was while Saul was still the king. (See 1 Samuel 16:1–13.) God had rejected Saul as king, though he continued to reign. Saul then became jealous of David and tried to kill him twenty-one times in nine years. David had several opportunities in which he could have killed Saul, but he didn't take them; David waited for God to give the kingdom to him. (See 1 Samuel 24.)

Jesus, at the river Jordan, in receiving the Holy Spirit, received the Father's words of commendation: *"This is My beloved Son, in whom I am well pleased"* (Matthew 3:17).

Just as David was tested for his kingship, so also was Jesus tested. (See Matthew 4:1.) The devil offered Jesus the kingdoms of this world, but Jesus rejected the offer because it did not come from the Father. When Jesus stood before Pilate, however, He told Pilate that He was born to be a king:

> *Pilate therefore said to Him, Are You a king then? Jesus answered, You say that I am a king. To this end was I born, and for this cause came I into the world, that I should bear witness to the truth. Every one that is of the truth hears My voice.* (John 18:37)

When Saul died, David was offered a part of the kingdom—only Judah. In 2 Samuel 2:4, men from Judah anointed David to be the king over the house of Judah. Actually, Saul's son was still king of the other tribes; though he was a very weak king. So it took some time for David to really prove himself qualified to be king over *all* of Israel.

Soon it will happen that Christ will receive His crown from His heavenly Father, and He will go forth to conquer. There is much to do; not all things are subject to Him. As a whole, the world has rejected Him, and they will accept, instead, the Antichrist:

I am come in My Father's name, and you receive
Me not: if another shall come in his own name,
him you will receive.   (John 5:43)

When David was anointed king over Judah, there was a long war between the house of Saul and the house of David, but at the end of seven years, David was made king over all Israel. (See 2 Samuel 5:1–3.)

At the end of the seven years of tribulation, the kingdoms of this world will become the kingdoms of Christ, and Jesus, too, will be crowned King of kings and Lord of lords at a great coronation.

After the coronation will follow the marriage supper of the Lamb, and Jesus will appear with His many crowns. Next, He will completely destroy the Antichrist and his armies. Then Satan will be chained in the bottomless pit for a thousand years, as recorded in chapter 20.

In Revelation 19:17, we see an invitation to the supper of God. In Revelation 16:13–14, under the sixth vial, we saw the unclean spirits, like frogs, lure the kings of the earth to this battle of the great day of God Almighty. In Revelation 19:17–18, they have reached their divine appointment. At the end of this battle, the birds will have a great feast on the dead bodies of those who will be slain there.

Joel spoke of this great battle:

———————————
———————————
———————————
———————————
———————————
———————————
———————————
———————————
———————————
———————————
———————————
———————————
———————————
———————————
———————————
———————————
———————————
———————————
———————————
———————————
———————————
———————————
———————————

Blow you the trumpet in Zion, and sound an alarm in my holy mountain: let all the inhabitants of the land tremble: for the day of the Lord comes, for it is near at hand; a day of darkness and of gloominess, a day of clouds and of thick darkness, as the morning spread upon the mountains: a great people and a strong; there has not been ever the like, neither shall be any more after it, even to the years of many generations. (Joel 2:1–2)

Joel called on Israel to repent:

Therefore also now, says the Lord, turn you even to Me with all your heart, and with fasting, and with weeping, and with mourning: rend your heart, and not your garments, and turn to the Lord your God: for He is gracious and merciful, slow to anger, and of great kindness, and repents Him of the evil. Who knows if He will return and repent, and leave a blessing behind Him; even a meat offering and a drink offering to the Lord your God? Blow the trumpet in Zion, sanctify a fast, call a solemn assembly: gather the people, sanctify the congregation, assemble the elders, gather the children, and those that suck the breasts: let the bridegroom go forth of his chamber, and the bride out of her closet. Let the priests, the ministers of the Lord, weep between the porch and the altar, and let them say, Spare Your people, O Lord, and give not Your heritage to reproach, that the heathen should rule over them: wherefore should they say among the people, Where is their God?

(Joel 2:12–17)

A northern army will descend on Israel, but it will be destroyed. Joel then wrote about the outpouring of the Holy Spirit on Israel:

And it shall come to pass afterward, that I will pour out My Spirit upon all flesh; and your sons and your daughters shall prophesy, your old men shall dream dreams, your young men shall see visions: and also upon the servants and upon the handmaids in those days will I pour out My Spirit. (Joel 2:28–29)

This prophecy was fulfilled in Acts 2:16–21 as the *former rain,* but the *latter rain* will be the outpouring of the Spirit at the end of the age, because it follows the great changes in the sun and the moon:

And I will show wonders in the heavens and in the earth, blood, and fire, and pillars of smoke. The sun shall be turned into darkness, and the moon into blood, before the great and the terrible day of the Lord come. (Joel 2:30–31)

God will gather the nations and plead with them:

For, behold, in those days, and in that time, when I shall bring again the captivity of Judah and Jerusalem, I will also gather all nations, and will bring them down into the valley of Jehoshaphat, and will plead with them there for My people and for My heritage Israel, whom they have scattered among the nations, and parted My land. (Joel 3:1–2)

Joel mentioned the valley of Jehoshaphat, which refers to the place of great victory for Jehoshaphat. (See 2 Chronicles 20.) God will show Himself mighty once again for His people, and He will fight for His people once again as He did for Jehoshaphat.

Joel looked back to that victory and looked forward to the deliverance Israel will have. Joel described how the Lord will judge these nations:

Let the heathen be wakened, and come up to the valley of Jehoshaphat: for there will I sit to judge all the heathen round about. (Joel 3:12)

This is described previously in Revelation:

And another angel came out of the temple which is in heaven, he also having a sharp sickle. And another angel came out from the altar, which had power over fire; and cried with a loud cry to him that had the sharp sickle, saying, Thrust in your sharp sickle, and gather the clusters of the vine of the earth; for her grapes are fully ripe. And the angel thrust in his sickle into the earth, and gathered the vine of the earth, and cast it into the great winepress of the wrath of God. And the winepress was trodden outside the city, and blood came out of the winepress, even to the horse bridles, by the space of a thousand and six hundred furlongs. (Revelation 14:17–20)

This is almost identical to Joel:

Put you in the sickle, for the harvest is ripe: come, get you down; for the press is full, the vats overflow; for their wickedness is great. Multitudes, multitudes in the valley of decision: for the day of the Lord is near in the valley of decision. The sun and the moon shall be darkened, and the stars shall withdraw their shining. The Lord also shall roar out of Zion, and utter His voice from Jerusalem; and the heavens and the earth shall shake: but the Lord will be the hope of His people, and the strength of the children of Israel. (Joel 3:13–16)

God spoke specifically of the great northern army that He will destroy. Ezekiel 38:2 NKJV mentions Russia, calling it *Rosh*, the army of the north. The beast rising out of the sea in Revelation 13 has feet like a bear. Russia is symbolized by a bear today.

Persia, in Bible prophecy, was also symbolized by a bear:

And behold another beast, a second, like to a bear, and it raised up itself on one side, and it had three ribs in the mouth of it between the teeth of it: and they said thus to it, Arise, devour much flesh.   (Daniel 7:5)

Persia will be a part of the Russian confederacy:

Persia, Ethiopia, and Libya with them; all of them with shield and helmet.   (Ezekiel 38:5)

Another symbol in Revelation 13 is the dragon. China, another great communist power, is symbolized today by the dragon.

Many times when God speaks of a *sickle*, He speaks of using nations as the rod of His power:

O Assyrian, the rod of My anger, and the staff in their hand is My indignation.   (Isaiah 10:5)

And another angel came out of the temple which is in heaven, he also having a sharp sickle. And another angel came out from the altar, which had power over fire; and cried with a loud cry to him that had the sharp sickle, saying, Thrust in your sharp sickle, and gather the clusters of the vine of the earth; for her grapes are fully ripe. And the angel thrust in his sickle into the earth, and gathered the vine of the earth, and cast it into the great winepress of the wrath of God. And the winepress was trodden outside the city, and blood came out of the winepress, even to the horse bridles, by the space of a thousand and six hundred furlongs. (Revelation 14:17–20)

The rod and the sickle will be instruments of God's judgment.

Red is the color of communism. Remember the beast is a scarlet-colored beast. Russia will be opposed when she tries to invade Israel:

Sheba, and Dedan, and the merchants of Tarshish, with all the young lions thereof, shall say to you, Are you come to take a spoil? have you gathered your company to take a prey? to carry away silver and gold, to take away cattle and goods, to take a great spoil? (Ezekiel 38:13)

When we compare this with Revelation 16, we see how they will be judged. First there will be a great earthquake:

And there were voices, and thunders, and lightnings; and there was a great earthquake, such as was not since men were upon the earth, so mighty an earthquake, and so great. (Revelation 16:18)

Second, there will be the fall of Babylon:

And the great city was divided into three parts, and the cities of the nations fell: and great Babylon came in remembrance before God, to give to her the cup of the wine of the fierceness of His wrath. (Revelation 16:19; see also Revelation 17 and 19)

Third, there will be the leveling of the mountains:

And every island fled away, and the mountains were not found. (Revelation 16:20)

Fourth, there will be the mighty hail from heaven:

And there fell upon men a great hail out of heaven, every stone about the weight of a talent: and men blasphemed God because of the plague of the hail; for the plague thereof was exceeding great. (Revelation 16:21)

Ezekiel also spoke of this great supper of God:

And, you son of man, thus says the Lord God; Speak to every feathered fowl, and to every beast of the field, Assemble yourselves, and come; gather yourselves on every side to My sacrifice that I do sacrifice for you, even a great sacrifice upon the mountains of Israel, that you may eat flesh, and drink blood. You shall eat the flesh of the mighty, and drink the blood of the princes of the earth, of rams, of lambs, and of goats, of bullocks, all of them fatlings of Bashan. And you shall eat fat till you be full, and drink blood till you be drunken, of My sacrifice which I have sacrificed for you. Thus you shall be filled at My table with horses and chariots, with mighty men, and with all men of war, says the Lord God. (Ezekiel 39:17–20)

The judgment of God upon Russia will open the eyes of His people:

And I will set My glory among the heathen, and all the heathen shall see My judgment that I have executed, and My hand that I have laid upon them. So the house of Israel shall know that I am the Lord their God from that day and forward. (Ezekiel 39:21–22)

REVELATION 19

¹⁷And I saw an angel standing in the sun; and he cried with a loud voice, saying to all the fowls that fly in the midst of heaven, Come and gather yourselves together to the supper of the great God;

¹⁸that you may eat the flesh of kings, and the flesh of captains, and the flesh of mighty men, and the flesh of horses, and of them that sit on them, and the flesh of all men, both free and bond, both small and great.

¹⁹And I saw the beast, and the kings of the earth, and their armies, gathered together to make war against Him that sat on the horse, and against His army.

²⁰And the beast was taken, and with him the false prophet that wrought miracles before him, with which he deceived them that had received the mark of the beast, and them that worshiped his image. These both were cast alive into a lake of fire burning with brimstone.

²¹And the remnant were slain with the sword of Him that sat upon the horse, which sword proceeded out of His mouth: and all the fowls were filled with their flesh.

NOTES

_____

_____

_____

The battle of Armageddon describes the destruction of the gentile image in Daniel 2: the stone that is cut without hands strikes the image in the feet and destroys it. (See Daniel 2:34.)

The prophecies that Israel has been waiting for will now be fulfilled. The kings of the world will want to take the spoil, and that spoil is Jerusalem:

Behold, the day of the LORD comes, and your spoil shall be divided in the midst of you. For I will gather all nations against Jerusalem to battle; and the city shall be taken, and the houses rifled, and the women ravished; and half of the city shall go forth into captivity, and the residue of the people shall not be cut off from the city. Then shall the LORD go forth, and fight against those nations, as when He fought in the day of battle. And His feet shall stand in that day upon the mount of Olives, which is before Jerusalem on the east, and the mount of Olives shall cleave in the midst thereof toward the east and toward the west, and there shall be a very great valley; and half of the mountain shall remove toward the north, and half of it toward the south…. And the LORD shall be king over all the earth: in that day shall there be one LORD, and His name one.
(Zechariah 14:1–4, 9)

And, you son of man, thus says the Lord GOD; Speak to every feathered fowl, and to every beast of the field, Assemble yourselves, and come; gather yourselves on every side to My sacrifice that I do sacrifice for you, even a great sacrifice upon the mountains of Israel, that you may eat flesh, and drink blood. (Ezekiel 39:17)

The outcome of this great battle of Armageddon is sure:

> And the beast was taken, and with him the false prophet that wrought miracles before him, with which he deceived them that had received the mark of the beast, and them that worshiped his image. These both were cast alive into a lake of fire burning with brimstone. And the remnant were slain with the sword of Him that sat upon the horse, which sword proceeded out of His mouth: and all the fowls were filled with their flesh. (Revelation 19:20–21)

CHAPTER TWENTY

¹And I saw an angel come down from heaven, having the key of the bottomless pit and a great chain in his hand.

²And he laid hold on the dragon, that old serpent, which is the Devil, and Satan, and bound him a thousand years,

³and cast him into the bottomless pit, and shut him up, and set a seal upon him, that he should deceive the nations no more, till the thousand years should be fulfilled: and after that he must be loosed a little season.

⁴And I saw thrones, and they sat upon them, and judgment was given to them: and I saw the souls of them that were beheaded for the witness of Jesus, and for the word of God, and which had not worshiped the beast, neither his image, neither had received his mark upon their foreheads, or in their hands; and they lived and reigned with Christ a thousand years.

⁵But the rest of the dead lived not again until the thousand years were finished. This is the first resurrection.

⁶Blessed and holy is he that has part in the first resurrection: on such the second death has no power, but they shall be priests of God and of Christ, and shall reign with Him a thousand years.

Satan will be in chains for a thousand years. This period is still a part of the end of the old world. The earth will be in ruins following the trumpet and vial judgments. It will require seven months to bury the dead:

And seven months shall the house of Israel be burying of them, that they may cleanse the land.
(Ezekiel 39:12)

The personal reconstruction will be under Christ's direction.

Now, in chapter 20, we are dealing with destiny. We need to look at the three places in the spirit world that are mentioned. Some have to do with temporary times, and some are permanent.

1. The *bottomless pit* in Revelation 17:8 is where the beast came from, and this will be Satan's prisonhouse for a thousand years:

And he laid hold on the dragon, that old serpent, which is the Devil, and Satan, and bound him a thousand years, and cast him into the bottomless pit, and shut him up, and set a seal upon him, that he should deceive the nations no more, till

⁷And when the thousand years are expired, Satan shall be loosed out of his prison,

⁸and shall go out to deceive the nations which are in the four quarters of the earth, Gog and Magog, to gather them together to battle: the number of whom is as the sand of the sea.

⁹And they went up on the breadth of the earth, and compassed the camp of the saints about, and the beloved city and fire came down from God out of heaven, and devoured them.

¹⁰And the devil that deceived them was cast into the lake of fire and brim-stone, where the beast and the false prophet are, and shall be tormented day and night for ever and ever.

NOTES

_____

_____

_____

_____

_____

_____

_____

_____

_____

_____

the thousand years should be fulfilled: and after that he must be loosed a little season.

(Revelation 20:2–3)

This is also where the locust demons originate:

And he opened the bottomless pit; and there arose a smoke out of the pit, as the smoke of a great furnace; and the sun and the air were darkened by reason of the smoke of the pit. And there came out of the smoke locusts upon the earth: and to them was given power, as the scorpions of the earth have power.   (Revelation 9:2–3)

2.   The *lake of fire* (Revelation 20:10) is where the beast and the false prophet were cast:

And the beast was taken, and with him the false prophet that wrought miracles before him, with which he deceived them that had received the mark of the beast, and them that worshiped his image. These both were cast alive into a lake of fire burning with brimstone.

(Revelation 19:20)

At the end of the thousand years, Satan will be thrown into the lake of fire also:

And the devil that deceived them was cast into the lake of fire and brim-stone, where the beast and the false prophet are, and shall be tormented day and night for ever and ever.

(Revelation 20:10)

3.   *Hades* is where the wicked human dead are confined. They are kept there until the time of judgment, and after the great white throne judgment, they are cast into the lake of fire:

*And death and hell were cast into the lake of fire.
This is the second death. And whosoever was not
found written in the book of life was cast into the
lake of fire.* (Revelation 20:14–15)

A great description is given of *hades* in Luke 16.

Another place mentioned is *tartaros* in the Greek,
and it is sometimes referred to as *hell*:

*For if God spared not the angels that sinned, but
cast them down to hell, and delivered them into
chains of darkness, to be reserved to judgment.*
(2 Peter 2:4)

This is a place of confinement for the wicked
angels only, and could be associated with the bottomless pit.

In the latter part of Revelation 19, when the
wicked are raised to stand before God in judgment
and their names are not found in the Lamb's book
of life, they are cast into the lake of fire. In the Old
Testament, it is called *Tophet*:

*For Tophet is ordained of old; yea, for the king
it is prepared; he has made it deep and large: the
pile thereof is fire and much wood; the breath of
the* Lord, *like a stream of brimstone, does kindle
it.* (Isaiah 30:33)

*And they have built the high places of Tophet,
which is in the valley of the son of Hinnom, to
burn their sons and their daughters in the fire;
which I commanded them not, neither came it
into My heart. Therefore, behold, the days come,
says the* Lord, *that it shall no more be called
Tophet, nor the valley of the son of Hinnom,
but the valley of slaughter: for they shall bury in*

Tophet, till there be no place.
(Jeremiah 7:31–32)

In the New Testament, it is called *Gehenna*, and was referred to by Jesus:

And fear not them which kill the body, but are not able to kill the soul: but rather fear Him which is able to destroy both soul and body in hell. (Matthew 10:28)

It had originally been prepared for the devil and his angels:

Then shall He say also to them on the left hand, Depart from Me, you cursed, into everlasting fire, prepared for the devil and his angels.... And these shall go away into everlasting punishment: but the righteous into life eternal.
(Matthew 25:41, 46)

The beast and the false prophet are cast there, and it is evident that they do not burn up, because they are still there when the devil is thrown into it a thousand years later:

And when the thousand years are expired, Satan shall be loosed out of his prison.... And the devil that deceived them was cast into the lake of fire and brim-stone, where the beast and the false prophet are, and shall be tormented day and night for ever and ever. (Revelation 20:7, 10)

The devil and his angels will not be permitted to interfere with God's program during the millennium. Revelation 20:4–6 concerns the saints sitting in judgment upon the nations:

Do you not know that the saints shall judge the world? and if the world shall be judged by you, are

you unworthy to judge the smallest matters?
(1 Corinthians 6:2)

Earlier, in chapter 4, we also saw the thrones of twenty-four elders:

And round about the throne were four and twenty seats: and upon the seats I saw four and twenty elders sitting, clothed in white raiment; and they had on their heads crowns of gold.
(Revelation 4:4)

The apostles were told that they would sit upon thrones during the regeneration:

And Jesus said to them, Verily I say to you, That you which have followed Me, in the regeneration when the Son of Man shall sit in the throne of His glory, you also shall sit upon twelve thrones, judging the twelve tribes of Israel.
(Matthew 19:28)

David will sit upon the throne of Israel:

And David My servant shall be king over them; and they all shall have one shepherd: they shall also walk in My judgments, and observe My statutes, and do them.   (Ezekiel 37:24)

In chapter one of Revelation, we read that *we* will be kings and priests unto God:

And has made us kings and priests to God and His Father; to Him be glory and dominion for ever and ever. Amen.   (Revelation 1:6)

The man child is spoken of as ruling the nations with a rod of iron:

And she brought forth a man child, who was to rule all nations with a rod of iron: and her child

_____

_____

_____

_____

_____

_____

_____

_____

_____

_____

_____

_____

_____

_____

_____

_____

_____

_____

_____

_____

_____

_____

_____

was caught up to God, and to His throne.
(Revelation 12:5)

Undoubtedly these are overcomers:

And he that overcomes, and keeps My works to the end, to him will I give power over the nations: and he shall rule them with a rod of iron; as the vessels of a potter shall they be broken to shivers: even as I received of My Father.
(Revelation 2:26–27)

And has raised us up together, and made us sit together in heavenly places in Christ Jesus: that in the ages to come He might show the exceeding riches of His grace in His kindness toward us through Christ Jesus. (Ephesians 2:6–7)

And he said to him, Well, you good servant: because you have been faithful in a very little, have you authority over ten cities. And the second came, saying, Lord, your pound has gained five pounds. And he said likewise to him, Be you also over five cities. (Luke 19:17–19)

The population of the earth will be drastically reduced:

And I will punish the world for their evil, and the wicked for their iniquity; and I will cause the arrogancy of the proud to cease, and will lay low the haughtiness of the terrible. I will make a man more precious than fine gold; even a man than the golden wedge of Ophir. (Isaiah 13:11–12)

And in that day seven women shall take hold of one man, saying, We will eat our own bread, and wear our own apparel: only let us be called

by your name, to take away our reproach.
            (Isaiah 4:1)

However, it will increase rapidly:

A little one shall become a thousand, and a small one a strong nation: I the LORD will hasten it in his time.   (Isaiah 60:22)

Of the increase of His government and peace there shall be no end, upon the throne of David, and upon his kingdom, to order it, and to establish it with judgment and with justice from hereafter even for ever. The zeal of the LORD of hosts will perform this.   (Isaiah 9:7)

The millennium will be a time of preparation for the earth be turned over to God:

Then comes the end, when He shall have delivered up the kingdom to God, even the Father; when He shall have put down all rule and all authority and power. For He must reign, till He has put all enemies under His feet. The last enemy that shall be destroyed is death.
            (1 Corinthians 15:24–26)

This phase of redemption of the earth will take a thousand years, but the kingdom will last forever:

For, behold, I create new heavens and a new earth: and the former shall not be remembered, nor come into mind. But be you glad and rejoice for ever in that which I create: for, behold, I create Jerusalem a rejoicing, and her people a joy. And I will rejoice in Jerusalem, and joy in My people: and the voice of weeping shall be no more heard in her, nor the voice of crying. There shall be no more there an infant of days, nor an

REVELATION 20

¹¹And I saw a great white throne, and Him that sat on it, from whose face the earth and the heaven fled away; and there was found no place for them.

¹²And I saw the dead, small and great, stand before God; and the books were opened: and another book was opened, which is the book of life: and the dead were judged out of those things which were written in the books according to their works.

¹³And the sea gave up the dead which were in it; and death and hell delivered up the dead which were in them: and they were judged every man according to their works.

¹⁴And death and hell were cast into the lake of fire. This is the second death. ¹⁵And whosoever was not found written in the book of life was cast into the lake of fire.

NOTES

_____

_____

_____

_____

_____

_____

_____

_____

old man that has not filled his days: for the child shall die a hundred years old; but the sinner being a hundred years old shall be accursed. And they shall build houses, and inhabit them; and they shall plant vineyards, and eat the fruit of them. They shall not build, and another inhabit; they shall not plant, and another eat: for as the days of a tree are the days of My people, and My elect shall long enjoy the work of their hands.
(Isaiah 65:17–22)

Revelation 20:7–10 records the final cleansing; after a thousand years, the final judgment is completed. Gog and Magog (Gog is Satan and Magog is whom Satan possesses) are devoured by fire from heaven.

In the great white throne judgment of verse 11, we see the judgment will be basically based upon works. Jesus spoke of this judgment:

But I say to you, That every idle word that men shall speak, they shall give account thereof in the day of judgment. For by your words you shall be justified, and by your words you shall be condemned. (Matthew 12:36–37)

There are two books present—one with works and one is the Book of Life.

The sheep and goat nations will be judged. (See Matthew 25:31–46.)

Finally, we see Isaiah's prophecy fulfilled:

The wilderness and the solitary place shall be glad for them; and the desert shall rejoice, and blossom as the rose. It shall blossom abundantly, and rejoice even with joy and singing: the glory of Lebanon shall be given to it, the excellency *of Carmel and Sharon, they shall see the glory of the* LORD, *and the excellency of our God....* Then shall the lame man leap as a hart, and the tongue of the dumb sing: for in the wilderness shall waters break out, and streams in the desert. And the parched ground shall become a pool, and the thirsty land springs of water: in the habitation of dragons, where each lay, shall be grass with reeds and rushes.* (Isaiah 35:1–2, 6–7)

CHAPTER TWENTY-ONE

We are now entering a new heaven and a new earth. I do not believe that this means that the old was totally wiped out. When the King James Version refers to the *end of the world*, it means to the end of the *age*. Peter tells us what the heavens and the earth go through during the tribulation period just prior to the day of the Lord:

> But the day of the Lord will come as a thief in the night; in the which the heavens shall pass away with a great noise, and the elements shall melt with fervent heat, the earth also and the works that are therein shall be burned up. Seeing then that all these things shall be dissolved, what manner of persons ought you to be in all holy conversation and godliness, looking for and hasting to the coming of the day of God, wherein the heavens being on fire shall be dissolved, and the elements shall melt with fervent heat?
>
> (2 Peter 3:10–12)

Peter said the antediluvian world *"perished,"* but the earth was not annihilated:

REVELATION 21

[1]And I saw a new heaven and a new earth: for the first heaven and the first earth were passed away; and there was no more sea.

[2]And I John saw the holy city, new Jerusalem, coming down from God out of heaven, prepared as a bride adorned for her husband.

[3]And I heard a great voice out of heaven saying, Behold, the tabernacle of God is with men, and He will dwell with them, and they shall be His people, and God Himself shall be with them, and be their God.

[4]And God shall wipe away all tears from their eyes; and there shall be no more death, neither sorrow, nor crying, neither shall there be any more pain: for the former things are passed away.

[5]And He that sat upon the throne said, Behold, I make all things new. And He said to me, Write: for these words are true and faithful.

[6]And He said to me, It is done. I am Alpha and Omega, the beginning and the end. I will give to him that is thirsty of the fountain of the water of life freely.

[7]He that overcomes shall inherit all things; and I will be his God, and he shall be My son.

[8]But the fearful, and unbelieving, and the abominable, and murderers, and whoremongers, and sorcerers, and idolaters, and all liars, shall have their part in the lake which

burns with fire and brimstone: which is the second death.

⁹And there came to me one of the seven angels which had the seven vials full of the seven last plagues, and talked with me, saying, Come here, I will show you the bride, the Lamb's wife.

¹⁰And he carried me away in the Spirit to a great and high mountain, and showed me that great city, the holy Jerusalem, descending out of heaven from God,

¹¹Having the glory of God: and her light was like to a stone most precious, even like a jasper stone, clear as crystal;

¹²and had a wall great and high, and had twelve gates, and at the gates twelve angels, and names written thereon, which are the names of the twelve tribes of the children of Israel:

¹³on the east three gates; on the north three gates; on the south three gates; and on the west three gates.

¹⁴And the wall of the city had twelve foundations, and in them the names of the twelve apostles of the Lamb.

¹⁵And he that talked with me had a golden reed to measure the city, and the gates thereof, and the wall thereof.

¹⁶And the city lies foursquare, and the length is as large as the breadth: and he measured the city with the reed, twelve thousand furlongs.

For this they willingly are ignorant of, that by the word of God the heavens were of old, and the earth standing out of the water and in the water: whereby the world that then was, being overflowed with water, perished.

(2 Peter 3:5–6)

The earth at that time was cleansed with water; at the end it will have a baptism of fire. It will be renewed—go back to its original owner—and be redeemed and regenerated as though born again for the ages of ages that are to come.

Christ is the King of the new Jerusalem. Jesus said, *"I go to prepare a place for you"* (John 14:2). For over nineteen hundred years, Jesus, the Builder and Architect of the new Jerusalem, has been busy. For every member of the church, there is a place prepared.

According to Revelation 21:9–27, the new Jerusalem will not be a part of the earth, but it will be near the earth. Its splendors will be tremendous. It will be 1,400 miles square, and 12,000 furlongs high. It's a cube, and it is foursquare. Its lighting will be the Lord; God will be its temple. It has a high wall, more than two hundred fifty feet high, and twelve gates. These gates are entrances for God's people to have access to the city. There are three gates on each of the four sides. It must be a gigantic city.

Each gate is guarded by an angel named after one of the tribes of Israel. (See Revelation 21:12.) These angels are present because of their relationship and work with man. It seems as though each of the tribes has an angel, just as each of the churches had an angel in Revelation 2 and 3.

It is interesting that the gates are made of pearl. (See Revelation 21:21.) A pearl is really a living organism. An oyster receives an injury because of a particle of sand that irritates it, and it gives off a fluid called *nacre*, which covers it again, and again, and again. Out of the injury of the oyster comes the pearl. Jesus had to be injured for our sin. But He was covered with righteousness. He is the pearl of great price. Those twelve gates will say to Israel that the pearl has become their most precious stone.

The twelve foundations are beautiful stones. (See Revelation 21:19–20.) They seem to be in layers, built upon each other, and they go completely around all four sides. Let's look at a description of these magnificent stones:

Jasper: gold in color and clear as glass

Sapphire: like a diamond, very hard but blue in color

Chalcedony: thought to be sky blue, an agate stone

Emerald: bright green

Sardonyx: red with some white flashes

Sardius: honey colored

Chrysolyte: golden and sometimes pale green

Beryl: sea green

Topaz: pale yellow

Chrysoprasus: light green

Jacinth: violet

Amethyst: purple

Remember, we are told that Abraham looked for a city:

By faith he sojourned in the land of promise, as in a strange country, dwelling in tabernacles with Isaac and Jacob, the heirs with him of the same promise: for he looked for a city which has

The length and the breadth and the height of it are equal.

17And he measured the wall thereof, a hundred and forty and four cubits, according to the measure of a man, that is, of the angel.

18And the building of the wall of it was of jasper: and the city was pure gold, like to clear glass.

19And the foundations of the wall of the city were garnished with all manner of precious stones. The first foundation was jasper; the second, sapphire; the third, a chalcedony; the fourth, an emerald;

20the fifth, sardonyx; the sixth, sardius; the seventh, chrysolyte; the eighth, beryl; the ninth, a topaz; the tenth, a chrysoprasus; the eleventh, a jacinth; the twelfth, an amethyst.

21And the twelve gates were twelve pearls; every several gate was of one pearl: and the street of the city was pure gold, as it were transparent glass.

22And I saw no temple therein: for the Lord God almighty and the Lamb are the temple of it.

23And the city had no need of the sun, neither of the moon, to shine in it: for the glory of God did lighten it, and the Lamb is the light thereof.

24And the nations of them which are saved shall walk in the light of it: and the kings of the earth do bring their glory and honor into it.

²⁵And the gates of it shall not be shut at all by day: for there shall be no night there.

²⁶And they shall bring the glory and honor of the nations into it.

²⁷And there shall in no wise enter into it any thing that defiles, neither whatsoever works abomination, or makes a lie: but they which are written in the Lamb's book of life.

NOTES

_____

_____

_____

_____

_____

_____

_____

_____

_____

_____

_____

_____

_____

_____

_____

_____

foundations, whose builder and maker is God. (Hebrews 11:9–10)

This will be consummated by Abraham and the sons of Abraham, who have received Jesus Christ the Messiah:

But you are come to mount Zion, and to the city of the living God, the heavenly Jerusalem, and to an innumerable company of angels, to the general assembly and church of the firstborn, which are written in heaven, and to God the Judge of all, and to the spirits of just men made perfect, and to Jesus the mediator of the new covenant, and to the blood of sprinkling, that speaks better things than that of Abel. (Hebrews 12:22–24)

Those who have rejected Jesus will not be admitted to this city:

And there shall in no wise enter into it any thing that defiles, neither whatsoever works abomination, or makes a lie: but they which are written in the Lamb's book of life. (Revelation 21:27)

CHAPTER TWENTY-TWO

At last, we enter heaven on earth. This is what God has prepared for those who love Him:

When the Bible opens, we see, in the first two chapters of Genesis, God's preparation of creation—the beautiful conditions on the earth that He prepared for man and woman. Now, at the end of Revelation, we see a heaven on earth that God has again established for man. In all of the Bible, God keeps the door open for men to come to Him freely, by faith, or reject Him by the rebellion of their own will.

In Genesis 3, man was forbidden to eat of the tree of life:

> And the LORD God said, Behold, the man is become as one of Us, to know good and evil: and now, lest he put forth his hand, and take also of the tree of life, and eat, and live for ever: therefore the LORD God sent him forth from the garden of Eden, to till the ground from where he was taken. So He drove out the man; and He placed at the east of the garden of Eden Cherubims, and a flaming sword which turned every way, to keep the way of the tree of life.   (Genesis 3:22–24)

REVELATION 22

¹And he showed me a pure river of water of life, clear as crystal, proceeding out of the throne of God and of the Lamb.

²In the midst of the street of it, and on either side of the river, was there the tree of life, which bore twelve manner of fruits, and yielded her fruit every month: and the leaves of the tree were for the healing of the nations.

³And there shall be no more curse: but the throne of God and of the Lamb shall be in it; and His servants shall serve Him:

⁴and they shall see His face; and His name shall be in their foreheads.

⁵And there shall be no night there; and they need no candle, neither light of the sun; for the Lord God gives them light: and they shall reign for ever and ever.

⁶And he said to me, These sayings are faithful and true: and the Lord God of the holy prophets sent His angel to show to His servants the things which must shortly be done.

⁷Behold, I come quickly: blessed is he that keeps the sayings of the prophecy of this book.

⁸And I John saw these things, and heard them. And when I had heard and seen, I fell down to worship before the feet of the angel which showed me these things.

⁹Then says he to me, See you do it not: for I am your fellow-servant,

and of your brethren the prophets, and of them which keep the sayings of this book: worship God.

¹⁰And he says to me, Seal not the sayings of the prophecy of this book: for the time is at hand.

¹¹He that is unjust, let him be unjust still: and he which is filthy, let him be filthy still: and he that is righteous, let him be righteous still: and he that is holy, let him be holy still.

¹²And, behold, I come quickly; and My reward is with Me, to give every man according as his work shall be.

¹³I am Alpha and Omega, the beginning and the end, the First and the Last.

¹⁴Blessed are they that do His commandments, that they may have right to the tree of life, and may enter in through the gates into the city.

¹⁵For outside are dogs, and sorcerers, and whoremongers, and murderers, and idolaters, and whosoever loves and makes a lie.

¹⁶I Jesus have sent My angel to testify to you these things in the churches. I am the Root and the Offspring of David, and the Bright and Morning Star.

¹⁷And the Spirit and the bride say, Come. And let him that hears say, Come. And let him that is thirsty come. And whosoever will, let him take the water of life freely.

¹⁸For I testify to every man that hears the words of the prophecy of this book, If any man shall add to

In Revelation, man is invited again to eat of the tree of life:

In the midst of the street of it, and on either side of the river, was there the tree of life, which bore twelve manner of fruits, and yielded her fruit every month: and the leaves of the tree were for the healing of the nations. (Revelation 22:2)

Chapter 22 has the great double invitation: the Spirit and the bride say, "*Come*" (verse 17).

There are severe warnings to anyone who takes away from the words of this prophecy:

For I testify to every man that hears the words of the prophecy of this book, If any man shall add to these things, God shall add to him the plagues that are written in this book: and if any man shall take away from the words of the book of this prophecy, God shall take away his part out of the book of life, and out of the holy city, and from the things which are written in this book. (Revelation 22:18–19)

To the faithful Christian, however, there is only the promise of blessing:

The grace of our Lord Jesus Christ be with you all. Amen. (Revelation 22:21)

How can we resist so great a salvation?

these things, God shall add to him the plagues that are written in this book:

¹⁹and if any man shall take away from the words of the book of this prophecy, God shall take away his part out of the book of life, and out of the holy city, and from the things which are written in this book.

²⁰He which testifies these things says, Surely I come quickly. Amen. Even so, come, Lord Jesus.

²¹The grace of our Lord Jesus Christ be with you all. Amen.

NOTES

BIBLIOGRAPHY

Arthur Bloomfield, *All Things New* (Minneapolis, MN: Bethany Fellowship, Inc., 1959).

Gordon Lindsay, *Revelation Series* (Dallas, TX: Christ for the Nations, Inc., 1962).

ABOUT THE AUTHOR

As founder and president of Marilyn Hickey Ministries, MARILYN HICKEY is being used by God to live the Word and unlock the miraculous. Her Bible-teaching ministry is an international outreach via television, satellite, books, CDs, DVDs, and healing meetings, often bringing the gospel to people who have never heard it before. One of the most respected and anointed Bible teachers in the world, she has developed a unique and powerful ability to communicate deep biblical truths in a way that is understandable and practical for everyday life. Her previous books with Whitaker House include *Spiritual Warfare, Total Healing,* and the 30 Meditations series. Her most recent title, *Revelation Project,* was a collaboration with artist Cynthia Stanchak. Marilyn and her late husband, Wallace Hickey, are the founding pastors of Encounter Church in Centennial, Colorado. They have two grown children, five grandchildren, and four great-grandchildren.

Welcome to Our House!

We Have a Special Gift for You

It is our privilege and pleasure to share in your love of Christian books. We are committed to bringing you authors and books that feed, challenge, and enrich your faith.

To show our appreciation, we invite you to sign up to receive a specially selected **Reader Appreciation Gift**, with our compliments. Just go to the Web address at the bottom of this page.

God bless you as you seek a deeper walk with Him!

WE HAVE A GIFT FOR YOU. VISIT:

whpub.me/nonfictionthx

WHITAKER
HOUSE